THE SMUGGLERS

CHASE OF THE "FOUR BROTHERS" BY THE "BADGER"

From a drawing by Lord Teignmouth.

THE SMUGGLERS

Picturesque Chapters in the History of Contraband

BY

LORD TEIGNMOUTH, COMMANDER R.N.
AND
CHARLES G. HARPER

"SMUGGLER.—*A wretch who, in defiance of the laws, imports or exports goods without payment of the customs.*"—DR. JOHNSON

ILLUSTRATED BY PAUL HARDY, BY THE AUTHORS, AND FROM OLD PRINTS AND PICTURES

VOL. I

EP Publishing Limited
1973

Copyright © 1973 Lord Teignmouth and Trustees of
F. J. Bourne deceased

Copyright © in reprint 1973 EP Publishing Limited
East Ardsley, Wakefield
Yorkshire, England

First published 1923 by Cecil Palmer, London

ISBN 0 85409 899 2

Please address all enquiries to EP Publishing Ltd.
(address as above)

Printed in Great Britain by
The Scolar Press Limited, Menston, Yorkshire

PREFACE

It seems well to introduce these volumes with an account of their history, for they have one. In the year 1892 Lord Teignmouth, at that time Commander the Honourable H. N. Shore, R.N., published a volume, SMUGGLING DAYS AND SMUGGLING WAYS, *the outcome of a long and professional acquaintance with the Coastguard Service and all the curious lore relating to past smuggling times which that intimate contact with the coast implies.*

In 1909 was published in one volume THE SMUGGLERS, *a work by myself. Both these volumes have long been out of print and not easy to obtain.*

During that interval, Lord Teignmouth and myself, with a common interest in those robustious old smuggling days, have corresponded and exchanged ideas, finally with this result, that the reader now has put before him two considerable volumes which do not aim at telling all that is to be told of those smuggling activities (for that would be impossible, short of, let us say, six volumes). But they do trace the doings of the " Free Traders " from the earliest times to the present with a fullness which, it is thought, will satisfy the general reader.

Hitherto, published matter, whether in the form of local guide-books or of fugitive articles, has been very largely composed of mere gossip and undocumented legend. In those pages every cave along the coast was a smugglers' cave, and every sinister-looking old house was full of their hiding-holes. All very well

PREFACE

in their way, no doubt, and none might dispute, just as none could produce evidence to prove the truth of those stories.

But in all that time when these very vague and hearsay stories were told and written, there existed a very great deal of material at hand for the use of those who needed but the industry to collect and arrange it, and so to produce something which should take these stirring incidents out of their obscurity and set the story of the smugglers upon a firm footing of history.

Lord Teignmouth's keen interest in all these doings, together with the advantages his professional status has given him, have resulted in the acquisition by him of a vast mass of official correspondence, placed at his disposal by the Admiralty. Many among the secret and confidential documents of the eighteenth century relating to smuggling, and never before accessible, were transcribed by him some years before it seemed good to the Admiralty authorities to destroy the original documents. Much of that correspondence is printed in these pages, or the information contained in it used. Therefore these chapters needs must be the sole repository of that first-hand and exclusive historical matter.

Mine is the responsibility for selecting and arranging from the great mass of this evidence which Lord Teignmouth and myself, in collaboration have here printed; for the final arrangements for publication he has confided to me, as the ultimate working partner in this joint undertaking.

CHARLES G. HARPER.

September, 1923.

CONTENTS

CHAPTER		PAGE
	INTRODUCTORY	1
I.	THE "OWLERS" OF ROMNEY MARSH, AND THE ANCIENT EXPORT SMUGGLING OF WOOL—THE GUINEA-SMUGGLERS	19
II.	GROWTH OF TEA AND TOBACCO SMUGGLING IN THE EIGHTEENTH CENTURY—REPRESSIVE LAWS A FAILURE	37
III.	TERRORISING BANDS OF SMUGGLERS—THE HAWKHURST GANG—ORGANISED ATTACK ON GOUDHURST—THE "SMUGGLERS' SONG"	50
IV.	THE "MURDERS BY SMUGGLERS" IN HAMPSHIRE .	92
V.	THE "MURDERS BY SMUGGLERS" (*continued*)—TRIAL AND EXECUTION OF THE MURDERERS—FURTHER CRIMES BY THE HAWKHURST GANG . . .	103
VI.	OUTRAGE AT HASTINGS BY THE RUXLEY GANG—BATTLE ON THE WHITSTABLE-CANTERBURY ROAD—CHURCH TOWERS AS SMUGGLERS' CELLARS—THE DRUMMER OF HURSTMONCEUX—EPITAPH AT TANDRIDGE—DEPLORABLE AFFAIR AT HASTINGS—A SHOOTING AFFRAY AND ITS SEQUEL—THE INCIDENT OF "THE FOUR BROTHERS"	116
VII.	FATAL AFFRAYS AND DARING ENCOUNTERS AT RYE, DYMCHURCH, EASTBOURNE, BO-PEEP, AND FAIRLIGHT—THE SMUGGLERS' ROUTE FROM SHOREHAM AND WORTHING INTO SURREY—THE MILLER'S TOMB—LANGSTON HARBOUR	139
VIII.	EAST COAST SMUGGLING—OUTRAGE AT BECCLES—A COLCHESTER RAID—CANVEY ISLAND—BRADWELL QUAY—THE EAST ANGLIAN "CART GAPS"—A BLAKENEY STORY—TRAGICAL EPITAPH AT HUNSTANTON—THE PEDDAR'S WAY	153

CHAPTER		PAGE
IX.	THE DORSET AND DEVON COASTS—EPITAPHS AT KINSON AND WYKE — THE "WILTSHIRE MOONRAKERS"—EPITAPH AT BRANSCOMBE—THE WARREN AND "MOUNT PLEASANT" INN	160
X.	CORNWALL IN SMUGGLING STORY—CRUEL COPPINGER—HAWKER'S SKETCH—THE FOWEY SMUGGLERS—TOM POTTER, OF POLPERRO—THE DEVILS OF TALLAND—SMUGGLERS' EPITAPHS—CAVE AT WENDRON—ST. IVES	169
XI.	TESTIMONY TO THE QUALITIES OF THE SEAFARING SMUGGLERS—ADAM SMITH ON SMUGGLING—A CLERICAL COUNTERBLAST—BIOGRAPHICAL SKETCHES OF SMUGGLERS—ROBERT JOHNSON, HARRY PAULET—WILLIAM GIBSON, A CONVERTED SMUGGLER	191
XII.	THE CARTER FAMILY, OF PRUSSIA COVE	203
XIII.	JACK RATTENBURY	218
XIV.	WHY THE BLOCKADE WAS ABOLISHED	233

LIST OF ILLUSTRATIONS

	PAGE
CHASE OF THE *FOUR BROTHERS* BY THE *BADGER* Frontispiece	
SLAB COVERING TOMB OF THE SLAVONIAN GUILD OF MERCHANTS	5

	FACING PAGE
THE OWLERS	20
THE OWLERS CHASE THE CUSTOMS OFFICERS INTO RYE	24
GOUDHURST CHURCH	66
"THE GENTLEMEN GO BY"	68
"TURNING THEIR FACES TO THE WALL"	72
A REPRESENTATION OF YE SMUGGLERS BREAKING OPEN YE KING'S CUSTOM HOUSE AT POOLE	92
CHATER, CHAINED IN YE TURFF HOUSE AT OLD MILLS'S. COBBY, KICKING HIM, AND TAPNER, CUTTING HIM CROSS YE EYES AND NOSE, WHILE HE IS SAYING THE LORD'S PRAYER. SEVERAL OF YE OTHER SMUGGLERS STANDING BY THE "RED LION," RAKE	96
	100
JOHN MILLS ALIAS SMOAKER, AND RICHD. ROWLAND ALIAS ROBB, WHIPPING RICHD. HAWKINS TO DEATH AT YE "DOG AND PARTRIDGE" ON SLENDON COMMON, AND JEREMIAH CURTIS, AND THOS. WINTER ALIAS COACHMAN, STANDING BY AIDING AND ABETTING YE MURDER OF THE SAID RICHD. HAWKINS	106
REMAINS OF THE "DOG AND PARTRIDGE," SLINDON COMMON, AND THE "SMUGGLERS' CELLAR"	108
THE DRUMMER OF HURSTMONCEUX	120
EPITAPH TO THOMAS TODMAN AT TANDRIDGE	122

LIST OF ILLUSTRATIONS

	FACING PAGE
A LANDING AT BO-PEEP	142
SMUGGLERS' TRACKS NEAR EWHURST	146
THE MILLER'S TOMB	150
LANGSTON HARBOUR	152
THE "GREEN MAN," BRADWELL QUAY	156
KITCHEN OF THE "GREEN MAN"	158
"THE LIGHT OF OTHER DAYS"	176
THE DEVILS OF TALLAND	184
"OFT, FROM YON SOLEMN AND BAT-HAUNTED TOW'R, THE SMUGGLERS ISSUE AT THE MIDNIGHT HOUR"	186
ESCAPE OF JOHNSON	196
JOHNSON PUTTING OFF FROM BRIGHTON BEACH	198
PRUSSIA COVE	208
IN A FRENCH PRISON	210
JACK RATTENBURY	220

THE SMUGGLERS

INTRODUCTORY

CUSTOMS dues and embargoes on imports and exports are things of immemorial antiquity, the inevitable accompaniments of civilisation and luxury; and the smugglers, who paid no dues and disregarded all prohibitions, are therefore of necessity equally ancient. Carthage, the chief commerical community of the ancient world, was probably as greatly troubled by the questions of customs tariffs and smuggling as was the England of George the Third. Without civilisation, and the consequent demand for the products of other lands, the smuggler's trade cannot exist. In that highly organised condition of so-styled civilisation which produces wars and race-hatreds and hostile tariffs and swollen taxation, the smuggler becomes an important person, to Governments a hateful figure, but not infrequently a beneficent being to the ill-provided—in all nations the most numerous class—to whom in former times he brought, at a reasonable price, and with much daring and personal risk, those comforts which, when they had paid toll to the Chancellor of the Exchequer, were all but unattainable.

We certainly hear of customs charges being levied in the reign of Ethelred, when a toll of one halfpenny was charged upon every small boat arriving at Billingsgate, and one penny upon larger boats, with sails; but mediæval customs duties would seem to have originated in the ancient custom of "purveyance," by which official purveyors to the King were authorised to take toll of whatever goods were required for the King's household use. Here, in passing, we may note the change that time has brought about in the meaning of "purveyor." He is now one who supplies in the sense of selling; whereas in his origin he was an official who seized without payment, and was detested accordingly; not merely by reason of the Royal exactions, but largely on account of that gross abuse of the system by which the favourites of Court and the great nobles were permitted to share in these purveyances. But in any case, under the early Norman sovereigns, it would have been practically impossible to pay in coin for goods taken on the scale this implied, for coinage was scarce, and exchange and barter were more usual. What then should the King give in exchange (if anything) for the wines and other commodities purveyed to him? Originally he gave nothing, except that he deigned to reign over the lieges. But by the time when the Court of the Exchequer was established, in the reign of Henry the First, money had grown less scarce, and in the meanwhile the exorbitant purveying had grown so scandalous that these customary dues were re-founded and newly styled "Prisage" and "Butlerage." These were chiefly on goods for exportation. A "prise" was settled to be the taking of one tun of wine out of every ten, with exemption for cargoes of less than ten tuns. A sum in cash was paid (20s.) to the importer on each tun taken. This is what is meant in old documents by "Rightful Prisage." There was an "Evil Prisage," which meant that

PRISAGE

sometimes the King would issue writs for officials to stay all incoming wines at ports named and to purchase them at a price fixed: a price commonly far below market value. Usually these were extortions far and above the needs of the Royal household, and were calculated robberies in which the household shared, for, having acquired goods far in excess of requirements, at an absurdly low price, they then proceeded to re-sell at a higher. By charter of June 17th, 1278, Edward the First declared the citizens and burgesses of the Cinque Ports to be free of prisages on wines, as they had contended to be their ancient right. Probably one of the privileges they enjoyed in consideration of their naval aid.

About the same time the prisage of wine was removed from the purveyors and placed under control of the King's butler—not with results more satisfactory to the merchants, who complained as before of "Evil Prisage." The sole difference seems to be that another set of rogues got the plunder.

But this was not "Butlerage." That was a separate and individual tax, dating from 1303, and levied under the "Merchants' Charter," whereby (*inter alia*) the wines of foreign merchants coming into this country were freed from prisage and their merchandise from purveyance, except at their being paid for at trade price. In consideration of this, a "Butlerage" of 2s. per cask was payable within forty days of landing. As the size of a cask had not been specified, the alien importers very soon saw that it was largely to their advantage to use the tun, of 252 gallons.

This preference given to alien traders infuriated Englishmen, and not infrequently the foreigners were severely treated in English ports. The ill-feeling was, in a sense, justifiable; because, while we were Free Traders the foreigners were Protectionists. Among the fraternities or companies of foreigners in those times trading to our ports was the "Guild of the Slavonians," whose headquarters were at Venice. So important was their business, both at Southampton and inland, and so lengthy in time were their journeys, that the Guild, about 1491, purchased at North Stoneham, five miles inland, and on the way to Winchester, a vault in the church for the burial of any of their number who might die in this country. It is conjectured that they secured this by an arrangement with the clergyman, who badly wanted money for repairing and enlarging his church. The vault was soon needed, for in 1499 highwaymen attacked the Slavonians' convoy between Southampton and Winchester and killed two of them. The "highwaymen" were probably revengeful Southampton merchants, or ruffians hired by them; for feeling ran very high; the more especially as these aliens were accustomed to present the King, for favours received and in prospect, with supplies of Gascon wine. The vault is covered by a slab bearing at its corners the symbols of the four evangelists. In the middle is the double-headed eagle of the Nemagna dynasty of Serbia, which lasted from 1150 to 1389, when it went out on the blood-stained field of Kossovo. The slab is on the chancel floor, and not easily to be seen, for some twenty-five years ago a wooden floor was placed on the paving for the purpose of raising the level. So that this historic relic should not be altogether forgotten, the Hampshire Field Club with the consent of the vicar, had a trap-door made in the platform above it.

'TUNNAGE AND POUNDAGE'

The cleavage between the olden Royal Household impositions and the era of customs duties levied for national, as distinct from personal, needs is found

Slab covering tomb of the Slavonian Guild of Merchants in the church of North Stoneham.

in the "Tunnage and Poundage" levy introduced in the reign of Edward the Third. This, as introduced, was a "temporary" measure, and was intended to provide money for the keeping of the seas. It was legalised on the authority (such as that then was) of Parliament. Two shillings a tun was charged on all imports of wine; and, in addition an *ad valorem* duty of $2\frac{1}{2}$ per cent. on all imports except wine. The "temporary" measure was always re-enacted, and "Tunnage and Poundage" remained with us, indeed, as the more usual customs dues, until the time of that Revolution of 1688, which ended the Stuarts and brought in William the Third, and, incidentally, great foreign wars and continually increasing customs imposts intended to pay for them. Thus, whatever the faults of the Stuarts, the end of their House and the installing of the Dutchmen and of the Hanoverians involved the country in vast enterprises of the warlike sort, and in a National Debt; and it, by the appalling exactions of the customs, elevated import smuggling from a more or less casual occupation into a profession and a fine art.

Inland smuggling, however (that is to say, the concealment of dutiable home-made commodities, *e. g.* whisky) took its rise a little earlier; for excise was not known in England until it was imposed by a Declaration of the House of Commons, October 8th, 1642. It was a tax copied from the Dutch "Excijs," and when newly established in the following year was referred to as the "Office of Excise, or New Impost."

Smuggling was ever principally an affair of the south and west coasts of England, for the obvious reason that these are the nearest seaboards to the Continent. But, at the same time, it would not be in order to suggest that a good deal of contraband trade did not pass on the eastern and other coasts. The foreign merchants were the earliest adepts at

FOREIGN TRADE GUILDS

the running of uncustomed goods into the country. They had it, or sought and achieved their gains in all ways. While some, under the "Merchants' Charter," brought in their wines and other goods at preferentially low rates, others, not content with that, smuggled; while other aliens, chiefly Italians, wealthy financiers preying upon the necessities of the King, lent money and in return secured the farming of the customs. England was not then a manufacturing country. In the thirteenth century the Hanse merchants, it has been stated, farmed the whole of the English customs; but they seem to have been undercut by the more rapacious Lucca Guild. The King was practically in pawn to these foreigners. "He who goes a-borrowing, goes a-sorrowing" is an adage eternally true; and the sovereigns of England, borrowing on the security of the customs, gave away for an inadequate return many valuable privileges. It was thus a kind of rough justice that the foreign farmers often should find their own countrymen running goods into the country in a clandestine manner, and thus evading their ill-gotten dues. A rougher sort of equilibrium was sometimes attained by enterprising bandits who raided the aliens' takings and made off with much booty. It was not a complete adjustment, because this was private brigandage and loot, and did not come into the monarch's exchequer. We find, for example, that in 1282 an assize was issued in Kent seeking to discover who were those that had harboured a bold bad person named Bushe, outlawed for having stolen a considerable sum of customs' money from the Lucca Guild. It does not seem that Bushe was taken, or that those who sheltered him were discovered.

8 THE SMUGGLERS

By 1308 the Italians had secured the entire customs dues of this country. Seething discontent was a feature of this time at the ports at the extortions alleged to be the practice of the customs farmers, who were permitted to override local established privileges, and also, incredible though it may seem, they had the power not only of assessing their own export transactions on the basis of traders domiciled here, but rated English merchants on an aliens' scale. A long and bitter contention began between financially embarrassed sovereigns and their executives and the legislatures; and in the meanwhile the citizens of the important town of Bristol, whose privilege, time out of mind, it had been to collect their own customs and render afterwards to the King, found themselves suddenly placed under a new authority whose object it was to collect higher dues. They broke out into revolt, although in the end obliged to yield to the superior force sent to quell them, and an infinity of trouble arose.

It is historically interesting here to note that the Cinque Ports, freed in the time of Edward the Confessor from prisage and all dues and duties upon goods, secured from Edward the First a confirmation of their liberties and privileges in these and all other respects. The original privileges and the confirmation of them were alike granted for a consideration: those ports supplying ships and men when called upon to aid the King in his wars. Those ancient charters are always assumed, and that of 1278 has often been quoted literally; but the parchments have disappeared. That they existed there is no doubt, for writs from the sovereign desiring certain persons and ports to cease from levying prisage upon the wines of Cinque Ports burgesses are extant.

CINQUE PORTS RIGHTS

They state that the Cinque Ports have been " quit of prisage, time out of mind." It was this ancient right which was, many centuries after, to form a specious argument of the Kentish and Sussex smugglers, and those of some parts of Essex and Norfolk (for Great Yarmouth and Brightlingsea also were limbs of the Cinque Ports), that in importing wines and spirits at any rate they were but exercising those liberties and privileges duly granted their ancestors and inalienable. They thus, as of right, sought to bring whatever they pleased, customs free, into the country, and declared themselves to be honest men and free traders. And as " free traders " they continued to style themselves to the end, wholly repudiating the derogatory title of " smugglers."

This argument, however, although at an early date it may have had some value, ceased to be effectual with the end of the special services rendered by those ports, and the contention, therefore, of the smugglers really then amounted to the assertion that a privilege must remain eternal, like the laws of the universe. It was an impossible argument.

Tunnage and poundage, instituted in the reign of Edward the Third, ran through the centuries until towards the close of the seventeenth century, and the farming of the customs kept those dues company almost as long, being abolished only in 1671. Meanwhile smuggling had become an art, a profession, and a trade all in one, calling forth enterprise, skill, resourcefulness and daring in increasing degree, and at a quite early period involving organisation of no mean order and on no despicable scale. The smugglers were led by men of undoubted strategic and tactical skill, and they had behind them capital, by whom supplied, in the various districts in which the bands of contrabandists roamed, never became known, and now never can be revealed.

The first customs dues, apart from the King's own arbitrary prisages and such imposts, date from 1688. It was a move towards consolidation, but (as we so often have found in these our times of troubles and discontents) it was not a journey towards easier conditions. Higher and ever higher dues meant that fostering of a frame of mind in which not only the smugglers considered themselves honest but persecuted traders, but in which they were regarded by perhaps the majority of the nation as men who risked liberty and life itself for the purpose of bringing goods to the poor man's door far more cheaply than grasping Governments would permit. The smugglers perhaps never thought of themselves in that pure Galahad way. They never adopted so high a moral tone, and very often indeed they were mere ruffians. But there comes inevitably a point in exactions beyond which it is not merely rash, but even criminal, for any Government to proceed, whatever its need of revenue, and it then becomes the bounden duty of men to stand up to and contend with imposts that hamper life at every turn.

According to an entry in the Excise and Treasury reports of 1685, which shows that it was desired to obtain a boarding-boat to examine vessels in the Downs, with a view to preventing the running of brandy, it is clear that illegal import was already considerable. Deal had, in fact, already engaged in that long and intensive career of smuggling for which it earned a great notoriety. It was just an open beach in a lone country when Julius Cæsar landed there, for the invasion of Britain, 55 B.C.; but it seems quite likely that the first import smuggler

WOOL EXPORT SMUGGLING 11

there came ashore at that time from one of his galleys. Waterside Deal arose first about 1660.

These pages will show that not only import, but also export smuggling was long continued in England, and not only so, but that the export smuggling, notably that of wool, was for centuries the most important, if not the only, kind. The prohibition of sending wool out of the kindgom was, of course, introduced with the object of fostering the cloth manufacture; but there are always two sides to any question, and in this case the embargo upon wool soon taught the cloth-workers that, in the matter of prices, they had the wool-growers at their mercy. By law they could not sell to foreign customers, or (later) only upon paying heavy dues; and the cloth-workers could therefore practically dictate their own terms. In this pitiful resort—an example of the disastrous effect of Government interference with trade—there was nothing left but to set the law at defiance, which the wool-growers and their allies, the " owlers," accordingly did, risking life and limb in the wholesale exportation of wool. It is the duty of every citizen to oppose bad laws, but this opposition of ill-conceived enactments creates a furtive class of men, very Ishmaelites, who, with their liberty, and even their lives, forfeit, are rendered capable, in extremity, of any and every enormity. Hence arose those reckless bands of smugglers who in the middle of the eighteenth century became highly organised and all-powerful in Kent, Sussex, and Hampshire, and, realising their power, developed into criminals of the most ferocious type. They were, properly regarded, the products of bad Government, the creatures brought into existence by a vicious system that took its origin in the coming of William the Third, the

"Deliverer," as history, tongue in cheek, styles him.

The growth of customs dues in the last years of the seventeenth century, and so onward, in a vicious progression until the opening years of the nineteenth, was not in any way owing to consideration for home traders, or to a desire for the protection of British industries. They grew exactly in proportion as the needs of the Government for revenue increased; and were the direct results of that long-continued policy of foreign alliances and aggressive interference in continental politics—that "spirited foreign policy" advocated even in our own times—which was introduced with the coming of William the Third. We did well to depose James the Second, but we might have done better than bring over his son-in-law and make him King; and we might, still more, have done better than raise the Elector of Hanover to the status of British sovereign, as George the First. Then we should probably have avoided foreign entanglements, at any rate, until that later era when increased intercourse between the nations rendered international politics inevitable.

Foreign wars, and the heavy duties levied to pay for them, brought about the enormous growth of smuggling, and directly caused all the miseries and the blood-stained incidents that make the story of the smugglers so "romantic." Glory is very fine, and stirs the pulses in reading the pages of history, but it is a commodity for which victorious nations, no less than the defeated, are called upon to pay in blood, tears, and privation.

With the great peace that, in 1815, succeeded the long and harassing period of continual war, the people naturally looked forward towards a time when

EVERYTHING TAXED

the excessively heavy duties would be reduced, and many articles altogether relieved from taxation. As a matter of fact, some of these duties scarce paid the cost of their collection, and simply helped to keep in office a large and increasing horde of officials. But the price of glory continues to be paid long after the laurels have faded; and not for many years to come were those imposts reduced.

Sydney Smith, writing in 1820 on the subject of American desire for a large navy, even then very manifest, warned the people of the United States of the nemesis awaiting such indulgence. " We can inform Jonathan," he said, " what are the inevitable consequences of being too fond of glory : Taxes upon every article which enters into the mouth, or covers the back, or is placed under the foot; taxes upon everything which it is pleasant to see, hear, feel, smell, or taste; taxes upon warmth, light, and locomotion; taxes on everything on earth, and the waters under the earth; on everything that comes from abroad, or is grown at home; taxes on the raw material, taxes on every fresh value that is added to it by the industry of man; taxes on the sauce which pampers man's appetite and the drug that restores him to health; on the ermine which decorates the judge and the rope which hangs the criminal; on the poor man's salt and the rich man's spice; on the brass nails of the coffin and the ribands of the bride; at bed or board, couchant or levant, we must pay. The schoolboy whips his taxed top; the beardless youth manages his taxed horse with a taxed bridle on a taxed road; and the dying Englishman, pouring his medicine, which has paid seven per cent., into a spoon that has paid fifteen per cent., flings himself back upon his chintz bed which has paid twenty-two per cent., makes his will on an eight-pound stamp, and expires in the arms of an apothecary who has paid a licence of a hundred pounds for the privilege of putting him to death. His whole property is then immediately taxed from two to ten per cent. Besides the probate, large fees are demanded for burying him in the chancel; his virtues are handed down to posterity on taxed marble; and he is then gathered to his fathers—to be taxed no more."

The real cost of military glory was aptly shown by a caricaturist of this period, who illustrated the general rise of prices consequent upon war in the following incident of an old country-woman buying a halfpenny candle at a chandler's shop :

" Price has gone up," said the shopkeeper curtly, when she tendered the money.

" What's that for, then ? " asked the old woman.

" On account of the war, ma'am."

" Od rot 'em ! do they fight by candle-light ? " she not unnaturally asked.

Housekeepers of the present day may well enter—although somewhat ruefully—into the humour of this simple story, for in the great and continued rise of every commodity since the great Boer War it is most poignantly illustrated for us. In short, the people who pay for the glory see nothing of it, and derive nothing from it.

How entirely true were those witty phrases of Sydney Smith we may easily guess from the mere rough statement that there were, in 1787, no fewer than 1,425 articles liable to duty (very many of them taxed at several times their market value), bringing in £6,000,000 a year.

In 1797 the customs laws filled six large folio volumes. The total number of Customs Acts prior

TAXED ARTICLES

to the accession of George the Third was 800, but no fewer than 1,300 were added between the years 1760 and 1813, and newer Acts, partly repealing and partly adding to older enactments, were continually being added to this vast mass of chaotic legislation down to the middle of the Victorian era, until even experts were frequently baffled as to the definite legal position of many given articles. Finally—it is typical of our English amateur way of doing things—in 1876, when so-called " Free Trade " had come in, and few articles remained customable, the customs laws were consolidated.

Many years before, at one swoop, Sir Robert Peel had removed the duties from four hundred different dutiable articles, leaving, however, many hundreds of others more or less heavily assessed.

In consequence of this relief from taxation, smuggling rapidly decreased, and the Commissioners of Customs were enabled to report : " With the reduction of duties, and the removal of all needless and vexatious restrictions, smuggling has greatly diminished, and the public sentiment with regard to it has undergone a very considerable change. The smuggler is no longer an object of general sympathy, as a hero of romance; and people are beginning to awaken to a perception of the fact that his offence is not only a fraud on the revenue, but a robbery of the fair trader. Smuggling is now almost entirely confined to tobacco, spirits, and watches."

No fewer than four hundred and fifty other dutiable articles were struck off the list in 1845, and the Cobdenite era of Free Trade, to which, it was expected, all other nations would speedily be converted, had opened.

" Free Trade," we are told, " killed smuggling."

It naturally killed smuggling so far as duty-free articles were concerned; but this all-embracing term of " Free Trade " is altogether a mockery and a delusion. There has never been—there is not now—complete Free Trade in this so-called free-trade country. Wines and spirits, tobacco, tea and coffee, cocoa and sugar, are not they in the forefront of the articles that render regularly to the Chancellor of the Exchequer? There have been, indeed, throughout all the years of the Free Trade era, some forty articles scheduled for paying customs duty on import into the United Kingdom. In the financial year 1921-2 they helped the revenue to the extent of £130,000,000. To this total foreign wines contributed, in round figures $2\frac{2}{3}$ millions sterling; spirits $11\frac{1}{2}$ millions; and tea $17\frac{1}{2}$ millions. At the same period, the Excise revenue from beer was £121,840,000, and from spirits £51,250,000. The greater part of these large sums represents the price of victory in the Great War 1914-18. Hence there is a recrudescence of smuggling, on a very large scale, of which the public in general know, and are told, nothing.

The romance of smuggling has very largely engaged the attention of every description of writer, but we do not hear so much of its commercial aspects, although it must be evident that for men to dare so greatly as the smugglers did with winds and waves and with the customs' forces, the possible gains must have been great. Time and again a cargo of tea or of spirits would be seized, and yet the smugglers be prepared with other ventures, knowing, as they did, that one entirely successful run would pay for perhaps two failures. When tea could be purchased in Holland at sevenpence a pound, and sold in England at prices ranging from 3s. 6d. to 5s.,

SMUGGLING PROFITS

and when tobacco, purchased at the same price, sold at 2s. 6d., it is evident that great possibilities existed for the enterprising free-trader.

As regards spirits, if we take brandy as an example, we find almost equal profits; for excellent cognac was shipped from Roscoff, in Brittany, from Cherbourg, Dieppe, and other French ports in tubs of four gallons each, which cost in France £1 a tub, and sold in England at £4. One of the ordinary smuggling luggers, generally built especially for this traffic, on racing lines, would hold eighty tubs.

On such a cargo being brought, according to preconcerted plan, within easy distance off-shore, generally at night, a lantern or other signal shown from cliff or beach by confederates on land would indicate the precise spot where the goods were most safely to be beached; and there would be assembled a sufficient company of labourers engaged for the job. A cargo of eighty tubs required forty men, who carried two each, slung by ropes over chest and back. According to circumstances, they marched in company on foot, inland; or, if the distance were great, they went on horseback, each man with a led horse, carrying three or four tubs in addition. These labourers, although not finally interested in the safe running of the goods, and not paid on any other basis than being hired for the heavy job of carrying considerable weights throughout the night, were quite ready and willing to fight any opponents that might be met, as innumerable accounts of savage encounters tell us. Besides these carriers, there were often, in case of opposition to the landing being anticipated, numerous "batsmen," armed with heavy clubs, to protect the goods.

The pay of a labourer or carrier varied widely, of

course, in different places, at different times, and according to circumstances. It ranged from five shillings to half a sovereign a night, and generally included also a present of a package of tea or a tub of brandy for so many successful runs. It is recorded that the labourers engaged for riding horseback, each with a led horse, from Sandwich, Deal, Dover, Folkestone, or Romney, to Canterbury, a distance of some fifteen miles, were paid seven shillings a night. The horses cost the smugglers nothing, for they were commandeered, as a general rule, from the neighbouring farmers, who did not usually offer any objection, for it was not often that the gangs forgot to leave a tub in payment. The method employed in thus requisitioning horses was quite simple. An unsigned note would be handed to a farmer stating that his horses were wanted, for some purpose unnamed, on a certain night; and that he was desired to leave his stables unlocked for those who would come and fetch them. If he did not comply with this demand he very soon had cause to regret it in the mysterious disasters that would shortly afterwards overtake him : his outbuildings being destroyed by fire, his farming implements smashed, or his cattle mutilated.

The farmers, indeed, were somewhat seriously embarrassed by the prevalence of smuggling. On the one hand, they had to lend their horses for the smugglers' purposes, and on the other they discovered that the demand for carriers of tubs and other goods shortened the supply of labour available for agricultural purposes, and sent up the rate of wages. A labourer in the pay of smugglers would often be out three nights in the week, and, with the money he received and with additional payment in kind, was in a very comfortable position.

CHAPTER I

THE "OWLERS" OF ROMNEY MARSH, AND THE ANCIENT EXPORT SMUGGLING OF WOOL—THE GUINEA-SMUGGLERS

THE earliest conflicts of interest between smugglers and the Government were concerned with the export of goods, and not with imports. We are accustomed to think only of the import smuggler, who brought from across Channel, or from more distant shores, the spirits, wines, tea, coffee, silks, laces, and tobacco that had never yielded to the revenue of the country; but before him in point of time, if not also in importance, was the "owler" who, defying all prohibitions and penalties, even to those of bodily mutilation and death, sold wool out of England and secretly shipped it at night from the shores of Kent and Sussex.

English wool had from a very early date been greatly in demand on the Continent. The England of those distant times was a purely agricultural country, innocent of arts, industries, and manufactures, except of the most primitive description. The manufacturers then exercised their skilled trades largely in France and the Low Countries; and, in especial, the cloth-weaving industries were practised in Flanders.

So early as the reign of Edward the First the illegal exportation of wool engaged the attention of the authorities, and an export duty of £3 a bag (in modern money) was imposed, soon after 1276. This was in 1298 increased to £6 a bag, then lowered and then again raised. English wool was then worth 1s. 6d. a pound.

In the reign of Edward the Third a strenuous attempt was made to introduce the weaving industries into England, and every inducement was offered the Flemish weavers to settle here and to bring their art with them. In support of this policy, the export of wool was, in various years, subjected to further restrictions, and at one time entirely forbidden. The royal solicitude for the newly cradled English weaving industries also in 1337 forbade the wearing of clothing made with cloth woven out of the country; but it is hardly necessary to add that edicts of this stringency were constantly broken; and in 1341 Winchelsea, Chichester, and thirteen other ports were named, whence wool might be exported on payment of a duty of 50s. a sack of twenty-six stone—*i. e.* 364 lb.

The interferences with the sale and export of wool continued, and the duty was constantly being raised or lowered, according to the supposed needs of the time; but nearly always with unforeseen and disastrous effects. The wool staple was removed to the then English possession of Calais in 1363, and the export of it absolutely forbidden elsewhere. The natural result, in spite of the great amount of smuggling carried on, was that in a long series of years the value of wool steadily fell; the cloth-makers taking advantage of the accumulation of stocks on the growers' hands to depress the price. In 1390 the growers had from three to five seasons' crops on hand, and the state of the industry had become such that in the following year permission to export generally, on payment of duty, was

THE OWLERS

conceded. This duty tended to become gradually heavier, and, as it increased, so proportionably did the " owling " trade.

The price of wool therefore declined again, and in 1454 it was recorded as being not more than two-thirds of what it had been a hundred and ten years earlier. The wool-growers, on the brink of ruin, petitioned that wool, according to its various grades, might not be sold under certain fixed prices; which were accordingly fixed.

But to follow, *seriatim*, the movements in prices and the complete reversals of Government policy regarding the export would be wearisome. We will, therefore, pass on to the Restoration of the monarchy, in 1660, when the export of wool was again entirely forbidden. Smuggling of it was in 1662 again, by the reactionary laws of the period, made a felony, punishable with death; yet the active smugglers, the rank and file of the owling trade, who performed the hard manual labour for wages, at the instigation of those financially interested, continued to risk their necks for twelvepence a day. The low price their services commanded is alone sufficient to show us that labour, in spite of the risks, was plentiful. Not only Kent and Sussex, but Essex, and Ireland as well, largely entered into this secret "stealing of wool out of the country," as the phrase ran; and "these caterpillars" had so many evasions, and commanded so many combinations and interests among those officials whose business it was to detect and punish, that few dared interfere: hence the readiness of the labourers to "risk their necks," the risk being, under the circumstances, small.

Indeed, readers of the adventures of these owling desperadoes and of the customs officers who hunted them will, perhaps, come to the conclusion that the risks on either side were pretty evenly apportioned, and they will see that the hunters not seldom became the hunted.

The experiences of one W. Carter, who appears to have been in authority over the customs staff in the Romney Marsh district towards the close of the seventeenth century, were at times singularly vivid. His particular "hour of crowded life" came in 1688, while he was engaged in an attempt to arrest a body of owlers who were shipping wool into some French shallops between Folkestone and New Romney.

Having procured the necessary warrants, he repaired to Romney, where he seized eight or ten men who were carrying the wool on their horses' backs to be shipped, and desired the Mayor of Romney to commit them, but, greatly to the surprise of this zealous officer, who doubtless imagined he had at last laid some of these desperate fellows securely by the heels, the Mayor of Romney consented to the prisoners being admitted to bail. Mr. Carter, to have been so ingenuously surprised, must have been a singularly simple official, or quite new to the business; for what Mayor of Romney in those days, when every one on the Marsh smuggled, or was interested financially in the success of smuggling, would dare not deal leniently with these fellows! Nay, it was even abundantly probable that the Mayor himself was financially committed in these ventures, and perhaps even among the employers of Mr. Carter's captives.

Romney was no safe abiding-place for Carter and his underlings when these men were enlarged; and they accordingly retired upon Lydd. But if they had fondly expected peace and shelter there they were woefully mistaken, for a Marshland cry of vengeance was raised, and a howling mob of owlers, ululating more savagely than those melancholy birds from whom they took their name, violently attacked them in that little town, under cover of night. The son of the Mayor of Lydd, well disposed to these sadly persecuted revenue men, advised them to further retire upon Rye, which they did the next morning, December 13th, pursued hotly across the dyke-intersected marshes, as far as Camber Point, by fifty furious men. At Guilford Ferry the pursuers were so close upon their heels that they had to hurriedly dismount and tumble into some boats belonging to ships lying near, leaving their horses behind; and so they came safe, but breathless, into Rye town.

At this period Calais—then lost to England— alone imported within two years 40,000 packs of wool from Kent and Sussex; and the Romney Marsh men not only sold their own wool in their illicit manner, but bought other from up-country, ten or twenty miles inland, and impudently shipped it off.

In 1698, the severe laws of some thirty years earlier having been thus brought into contempt, milder penal enactments were introduced, but more stringent conditions than ever were imposed upon the collection and export of this greatly vexed commodity, and the civil deterrents of process and fine, aimed at the big men in the trade, were strengthened. A law was enacted (9 & 10 William the Third, c. 40, ss. 2 and 3) by which no person living within fifteen miles of the sea in the counties of Kent and Sussex should buy any wool before he became responsible in a legal bond, with sureties, that none of the wool he should buy should be sold by him to any persons within fifteen miles of the sea; and growers of wool in those counties within ten miles of the coast were obliged, within three days of shearing, to account for the number of fleeces shorn, and to state where they were stored.

The success of this new law was not at first very marked, for the means of enforcing it had not been provided. To enact repressive edicts, and not to provide the means of their being respected, was as unsatisfactory as fighting the wind. The Government, viewing England as a whole, appointed under the new Act seventeen surveyors for nineteen counties, with 299 riding-officers: a force barely sufficient for Kent and Sussex alone. It cost £20,000 a year, and never earned its keep.

Henry Baker, supervisor for Kent and Sussex, writing on April 25th, 1699, to his official chiefs, stated that there would be shorn in Romney Marsh, quite apart from the adjacent levels of Pett, Camber, Guilford, and Dunge Marsh, about 160,000 sheep, whose fleeces would amount to some three thousand packs of wool, "the greatest part whereof will immediately be sent off hot into France—it being so designed, preparations in great measure being already made for that purpose."

In fact, the new law at first did nothing more than to give the owlers some extra trouble and expense in cartage of their packs; for, in order to legally evade the extra disabilities it imposed, it was only necessary to cart them fifteen miles inland and make fictitious sale and re-sale of them there; thence shipping them as they pleased.

THE OWLERS CHASE THE CUSTOMS OFFICERS INTO RYE

DECLINE OF WOOL SMUGGLING 25

By this time the exportation of wool had become not only a kingly concern—it had aroused the keen interest of the nation at large, fast becoming an industrial and cloth-weaving nation. For two centuries and more past the cloth-workers had been growing numerous, wealthy, and powerful, and they meant, as far as it was possible for them to do, to starve the continental looms out of the trade, for sheer lack of material. No one cared in the least about the actual grower of the wool, whether he made a loss or a profit on his business. It is obvious that if export of it could have been wholly stopped, the cloth-workers, in the forced absence of foreign buyers, would have held the unfortunate growers in the hollow of their hands, and would have been able to dictate the price of wool.

It is the inalienable right of every human being to fight against unjust laws; only we must be sure they are unjust. Perhaps the dividing-line, when self-interest is involved, is not easily to be fixed. But there can be no doubt that the wool-growers were labouring under injustice, and that they were entirely justified in setting those laws at naught which menaced their existence.

However, by December 1703 Mr. Baker was able to give his superiors a more favourable report. He believed the neck of the owling trade to have been broken and the spirit of the owlers themselves to have been crushed, particularly in Romney Marsh. There were not, at that time, he observed, "many visible signs" of any quantities of wool being exported : which seems to us rather to point to the perfected organisation of the owling trade than to its being crushed out of existence.

"But for fine goods," continued the supervisor,

"as they call them (viz. silks, lace, etc.) I am well assured that the trade goes on through both counties, though not in such vast quantities as have been formerly brought in—I mean in those days when (as a gentleman of estate in one of the counties has within this twelve months told me) he has been att once, besides at other times, at the loading of a wagon with silks, laces, etc., till six oxen could hardly move it out of the place. I doe not think that the trade is now so carried on as 'twas then."

Things being so promising in the purview of this simple person, it seemed well to him to suggest to the Commissioners of the Board of Customs that a reduction of the annual charge of £4,500 for the preventive service along the coasts of Kent and Sussex might be effected. At that time there were fifty preventive officers patrolling over two hundred miles of seaboard, each in receipt of £60 per annum, and each provided with a servant and a horse, to help in night duty, at an estimated annual cost of £30 for each officer.

We may here legitimately pause in surprise at the small pay for which these men were ready to endure the dangers and discomforts of such a service; very real perils and most unmistakable disagreeables, in midst of an almost openly hostile country-side.

Mr. Baker, sanguine man that he was, proposed to abolish the annual £30 allowance to each of these hard-worked men for servant and horse, thus saving £1,500 a year, and to substitute for them patrols of the Dragoon regiments at that time stationed in Kent. These regiments had been originally placed there in 1698 to overawe the owlers and other

PATROLS IN ROMNEY MARSH 27

smugglers, the soldiers being paid twopence extra a day (which certainly did not err upon the side of extravagance) and the officers in proportion: the annual cost on that head amounting to £200 per annum. This military stiffening of the civil force employed to prevent clandestine export and import appears to have been discontinued in 1701, after about two years' experiment.

These revived patrols, at a cost of £200, the supervisor calculated, would more efficiently and economically undertake the work hitherto performed by the preventive officers' horses and men, still leaving a saving of £1,300 a year. With this force, and a guard of cruisers offshore, he was quite convinced that the smuggling of these parts would still be kept under.

But alas for these calculations! The economy thus effected on this scheme, approved of and put into being, was altogether illusory. The owling trade, of which the supervisor had supposed the neck to be broken, flourished more impudently than before. The Dragoons formed a most inefficient patrol, and worked ill with the revenue officers, and, in short, the Revenue lost annually many more thousands of pounds sterling than it saved hundreds. When sheriffs and under-sheriffs could be, and were, continually bribed, it is not to be supposed that Dragoons, thoroughly disliking such an inglorious service as that of chasing smugglers along muddy lanes and across country intricately criss-crossed with broad dykes rarely to be jumped, would be superior to secret advances that gave them much more than their miserable twopence a day.

Transportation for wool-smugglers who did not

pay the fines awarded against them was enacted in 1717; ineffectually, for in 1720 it was found necessary to issue a proclamation enforcing the law; and in five successive years from 1731 the cloth-workers are found petitioning for greater vigilance against the continued clandestine exportation, alleging a great decay in the woollen manufactures owing to this illegal export; 150,000 packs being shipped yearly. "It is feared," said these petitioners, fighting for their own hand, regardless, of course, of other interests, "that some gentlemen of no mean rank, whose estates border on the sea-coast, are too much influenced by a near, but false, prospect of gain:" to which the gentlemen in question, being generally brought up on the dead classic languages, might most fairly have replied, had they cared to do so, with the easy Latinity of *Tu quoque!*

This renewed daring and enterprise of the Sussex smugglers led to many encounters with the customs officers. Among these was the desperate engagement between sixty armed smugglers and customs men at Ferring, on June 21st, 1720, when William Goldsmith, of the Customs, had his horse shot under him.

A humorous touch, so far at least as the modern reader of these things is concerned, is found in the Treasury warrant issued about this time, for the sum of £200, for supplying a regiment with new boots and stockings; their usual allowance of these indispensable articles having been "worn out in the pursuit of smugglers."

In spite of all attempts to suppress these illegal activities, it had to be acknowledged, in the preamble of an Act passed in 1739, that the export of wool was "notoriously continued."

SILK AND SPIRITS SMUGGLING 29

The old-established owling trade of Romney Marsh at length, after many centuries, gave place to the clandestine import of silks, tea, spirits, and tobacco; but it was only by slow and insensible degrees that the owlers' occupation dwindled away, in the lessening foreign demand for English wool. The last was not heard of this more than five-centuries-old question of the export of wool, that had so severely exercised the minds of some twenty generations, and had baffled the lawgivers in all that space of time, until the concluding year of the final wars with France at the beginning of the nineteenth century.

Many other articles were at the same time forbidden to be exported; among them Fuller's-earth, used in the manufacture of cloth, and so, of course, subject to the same interdict as wool. A comparatively late Exchequer trial for the offence of exporting Fuller's-earth was that of one Edmund Warren, in 1693. Fortunately for the defendant, he was able to show that what he had exported was not Fuller's-earth at all, but potter's clay.

The headquarters of the smuggling trade with the Continent during the Napoleonic wars may be said to have been at Deal and Folkestone—small and unimportant places before the railway-spider spread its web over the land, and inhabited chiefly by smugglers, whose patrons—often influential people whose sources of wealth were but dimly suspected—resided, for the most part, inland, where the enormous depots, used in former times for the reception of contraband, had given place to less obtrusive "hides," whose sacred precincts were jealously guarded from prying eyes.

A curious feature of those stirring days was the

practice, adopted by everyone engaged in "the trade," of assuming a *nom de guerre*—" the names their godfathers and godmothers gave them never being breathed amongst them," says an old writer. The quaintness of these nicknames may be inferred from the titles by which two Dover smugglers were known to their friends : viz. " Cold-toast " and " Blow-the-bellows." It was remarkable, too, that, although a sort of fellowship was kept up amongst the whole body, yet a very marked distinction, we are assured, prevailed between the " runners " of the three ports, Deal, Dover, and Folkestone; and it was no difficult matter to tell which place a professor hailed from.

During the war with France, both Deal and Folkestone acquired a most unenviable notoriety in connection with " guinea smuggling "; and the activity with which this business was conducted by these two villages—for they merited no higher appellation at that time—might well be deemed incredible were not the facts well authenticated.

Captain Brenton tells us that, after the restrictions on cash payments by the Banks another species of smuggling commenced, with more than the usual spirit of enterprise. Boats of forty feet or more in length, on a breadth of six and a half and seven feet, rowed by twenty-four or thirty-six men, were continually employed in carrying specie from Dover to Calais. They were called " guinea-boats," and their rate of rowing in a calm was from seven to nine miles an hour, so that it was extremely difficult to take them. The boats for this traffic having been prohibited to be built in England, these artists carried on their employments on the pier of Calais, where our author saw many of them at work.

GUINEA SMUGGLING

It was stated in an official document emanating from the Royal Courts of Guernsey, dated 1800, that "there is no doubt that from ten to twelve thousand guineas are every week carried by the smugglers to the Continent."

To what use was this specie applied? "In the beginning of last century it is well known that the French Government was supplied with English gold to pay the troops who were fighting against us in the Peninsular War." But let us go to the fountain-head. "Explaining how he raised money for carrying on his wars," observes Barry O'Meara (*Napoleon at St. Helena*), "Napoleon said : 'I did not receive money direct from Spain. I got bills upon Vera Cruz, which certain agents sent by circuitous routes, by Amsterdam, Hamburg, and other places, to London, as I had no direct communication. The bills were discounted by merchants in London, to whom ten per cent., and sometimes a premium, was paid as their reward. Bills were then given by them upon different bankers in Europe, for the greater part of the amount, and the remainder in gold, which last was brought over to France by the smugglers. Even for equipping my last expedition after my return from Elba, a great part of the money was raised in London.'"

And yet the "Tyrant of Europe" was wont to attribute the antagonism to him throughout the Continent to Pitt and English gold!

Southey, in his *History of the Peninsular War*, tells us that the first intelligence Napoleon obtained of Massena's condition after he advanced to the lines of Torres Vedras, was brought from London by persons employed in smuggling guineas to the Continent.

Captain Boteler, R.N., in his interesting reminiscences, states that when he was lying in the Downs, as guardship, in the *Orontes* frigate, in 1815, guinea-smuggling was carried on with great daring, in eight-oared galleys specially built for the purpose. "We kept a sharp look-out," he adds, "and used to slip our cable at a moment's notice; but it was like sending a cow after a hare. Notwithstanding our shot, they would pull in the wind's eye and escape with the greatest ease."

In this curious business the Folkestone smugglers played a leading, perhaps the most distinguished, part; as stated in a work, descriptive of old Folkestone, published as late as 1856. We are told that "although the chief trade of the place was ostensibly its fisheries, the inhabitants were extensively engaged in smuggling both spirits and tobacco, as well as guineas, and derived the chief portion of their wealth from this source. First-rate luggers and other vessels, oftentimes of considerable size, and of fast-sailing or rowing properties, were built especially for the traffic. So openly was the smuggling carried on, that the owners of the contraband freights are known to have boldly selected their own goods on the beach in broad daylight. . . . The supply of gold for the French troops during the war was the most lucrative of the illicit trade." And in another work of a similar nature, published in 1846, the writer observes: "It is a fact so thoroughly well known, so constantly alluded to, and so frequently commented upon, as not to permit of its passing unnoticed, that many of the inhabitants of Folkestone, in common with other places on this coast, even persons of wealth and general good reputation, untainted with aught

DIGGING UP BURIED KEGS 33

deemed approaching to crime, were, for some years, during the long war with France, much engaged in private communications with the opposite coast."

In face of these admissions, it is amusing to find a local writer, in the year 1823, when smugglers were among the most familiar objects of the Folkestone shore, extolling his fellow-townsmen in these glowing terms: "It cannot be a circumstance of indifference to anyone who visits the town of Folkestone to know that its inhabitants are proverbially of a friendly disposition; and always found to possess the true spirit of independence and innate principles of honour which embellish the character of Englishmen."

Turner, who visited the south-east coast about this time, was so impressed with the Folkestoner's "innate principles of honour" that, in two of his drawings, executed hereabouts, he has imparted touches of local colouring that do credit to his powers of observation by accurately reflecting the "true spirit of independence" so dear to natives of the place. Thus, in one spirited drawing, a party of these honourable gentlemen are depicted carrying their wares over the cliff, just to the westward of the town; while in another we are shown the "informer" giving proof of the "innate principle of honour which embellished the character of Englishmen," by directing a party of officers to the spot where his confederates had buried their goods, in Eastware Bay.

We are indebted to a resident of Sandgate for a further curious picture of those times, displayed in extracts from a manuscript compiled by a Quaker who lived at Folkestone about the year 1820 : "Not a rush is Lord Liverpool or his angry philippic against Folkestone cared for. He may go on to 'wish Folkestone blotted from the map of Kent, that it was sunk in the sea, or gone to the d——l, because a detestable nest of smugglers.'

"Now, I could tell his Lordship that a more harmless, mild and innocent-looking set of gentlemen (I speak not of the men but of their masters) are not to be found in Christendom; and, what must (to be sure) be allowed to be paradoxical, a more loyal body of subjects our sovereign Lord the King has not got to his back.

"A great man once said of his enemy, 'that man will never forgive the injury he has done me'; but from the bottom of their hearts do they freely forgive all the injury which they have done both to George ye 3rd and 4th, or their revenues. They do not (like the squeamish Society of Friends) put to each other the following query, 'Art thou clear of defrauding the King of his Customs duties, or excises, or in dealing or using in goods suspected to be run?' Of the word 'defrauding' they cannot approve, for they think it worse than useless, because it savours of something like an ostentatious display of political honesty."

And he further remarks : "Some articles, owing to the badness of quality, are eventually dearer than if purchased at the legal market. But the good people of these parts do not think so, for, with them, 'stolen waters are sweet, and bread eaten in secret is pleasant.'"

Doubtless it was the recollection of these golden days that inspired Ruskin to pen that rhapsody which has become a classic of English literature.

SMUGGLING FOLKESTONE 35

"My attention has been directed to the letter headed—'A PEEP AT OLD FOLKESTONE,' to which I can only reply that, as New Folkestone has sold all that was left of Old Folkestone to the service of Old Nick—in the multiform personality of the South Eastern Railway Company—charges me a penny every time I want to look at the sea from the old pier, and allows itself to be blinded for a league along the beach by smoke more black than thunder-clouds, I am not in the least minded to present New Folkestone with any peeps and memories of the shore it destroyed, or the harbour it has filled and polluted, and the happy and simple life it has rendered for ever in the dear old town impossible."

It will gratify the reader to learn that, in 1823—when it was still possible to live " the happy simple life " so dear to Ruskin—and the smugglers—there existed, by way of antidote to all this happiness and simplicity, a " Society for conversation and debate on literary and moral subjects, with weekly meetings." This was quite as it should be; and fancy revels in the picture of those ripe scholars, who dealt in gin and dry goods, flocking in, to participate in the " feast of reason and flow of soul " dispensed at the weekly reunions.

There is a lingering tradition in the town that the services rendered by certain of its citizens during the war with France are still gratefully cherished by the financial houses concerned—which is only right and proper.

A memorial of the days so pathetically alluded to by Ruskin may be seen in the north-west corner of the parish churchyard, near the entrance, in the form of a headstone marking the resting-place of a young officer employed on Preventive service, bearing the following inscription :

<blockquote>
Sacred
to the memory of
EDWARD LAMPEN
late Admiralty Midshipman
of his Majesty's ship *Severn*,
age 23.
</blockquote>

This meritorious and promising young officer was interred here with military honours, having been drowned in the harbour of Folkestone when in the zealous execution of his duty, on the night of Sunday, 21st January, 1819.

<blockquote>Love'd—Honor'd—Lamented.</blockquote>

CHAPTER II

GROWTH OF TEA AND TOBACCO SMUGGLING IN THE EIGHTEENTH CENTURY—REPRESSIVE LAWS A FAILURE

SIDE by side with the export smuggling of wool, the import smuggling of tobacco and tea grew and throve amazingly in later ages. Every one, knowingly or unsuspectingly, smoked tobacco and drank tea that had paid no duty.

" Great Anna " herself, who was among the earliest to yield to the refining influence of tea—

> Great Anna, whom three realms obey,
> Doth sometimes counsel take, and sometimes tay—

in all probability often drank tea which had contributed nothing to the revenue. Between them tea and tobacco, in the illegal landing of the goods, found employment for hundreds of hardy seafaring men and stalwart landsmen, and led to much violence and bloodshed, beside which the long-drawn annals of the owlers seem almost barren of incident.

Early in the eighteenth century, when continental wars of vast magnitude were in progress, the list of dutiable articles began to grow quickly, and concurrently with the growth of this list the already existing tariff was continually increased. The smugglers' trade grew with these growths, and for the first time became a highly organised and widely distributed trade, involving every class. The time had come at last when every necessary of daily use was taxed heavily, often far above its ordinary trading value; and an absurd, and indeed desperate, condition of affairs had been reached, in which people of all ranks were more or less faced with the degrading dilemma of being unable to afford many articles generally consumed by persons of their station in life, or of procuring them of the smugglers—the "free traders," as they rightly styled themselves—often at a mere one-third of the cost to which they would have been put had their illicit purchasers paid duty.

The Government was, as we now perceive, in the mental perspective afforded by lapse of time, in the clearly indefensible position of heavily taxing the needs of the country, and of making certain practices illegal that tended to supply those needs at much lower rates than those thus artificially created, and yet of being unable to provide adequate means by which these generally detested laws could be enforced. It was, and is, no defence to hold that the revenues thus hoped for were a sufficient excuse. To create an artificial restraint of trade, to elevate trading in spite of restraint into a crime, and yet not to provide an overmastering force that shall secure obedience, if not in one sense respect, for those unnatural laws, was in itself a course of action that any impartial historian might well hold to be in itself criminal; for it led to continual disturbances throughout the country, with appalling violence, and great loss of life, in conflict, or in the darker way of secret murder.

But no historian would, on weighing the evidence available, feel altogether sure of so sweeping an indictment of the eighteenth-century governance of England. It was corrupt, it was self-seeking, it had

REPRESSIVE ACTS

no breadth of view; but the times were well calculated to test the most Heaven-sent statesmanship. The country, as were all other countries, was governed for the classes; and governed, as one would conduct a business, for revenue; whether the revenue was to be applied in conducting foreign wars, or to find its way plentifully into the pockets of placemen, does not greatly matter. This misgovernment was a characteristic failing of the age; and it must, moreover, be recognised that the historian, with his comprehensive outlook upon the past, spread out, so to speak, map-like to his gaze, has the advantage of seeing these things as a whole, and of criticising them as such; while the givers and administrators of laws were under the obvious disadvantages of each planning and working for what they considered to be the needs of their own particular period, with those of the future unknown, and perhaps uncared for. That there were some few among those in authority who wrought according to their lights, however feeble might be their illumination, must be conceded even to that age.

At the opening of this era, when Marlborough's great victories were yet fresh, and when the cost of them and of other military glories was wearing the country threadbare, the most remarkable series of repressive Acts, directed against smuggling, began. Vessels of very small tonnage and light draught being found peculiarly useful to smugglers, the use of such, even in legalised importing, was strictly forbidden, and no craft of a lesser burthen than fifteen tons was permitted. This provision, it was fondly conceived, would strike a blow at smuggling, by rendering it impossible to slip up narrow and shallow waterways; but this pious expectation was doomed to disappointment, and the limit was accordingly raised to thirty tons; and again, in 1721, to forty tons. At the same time, the severest restrictions were imposed upon boats, in order to cope with the ten, or even twelve and fourteen-oared galleys, rowed by determined " free-traders."

To quote the text of one among these drastic ordinances :

" Any boat built to row with more than four oars, found upon land or water within the counties of Middlesex, Surrey, Kent, or Sussex, or in the river Thames, or within the limits of the ports of London, Sandwich, or Ipswich, or any boat rowing with more than six oars found either upon land or water, in any other port, or within two leagues of the coast of Great Britain, shall be forfeited, and every person using or rowing in such boat shall forfeit £40."

These prohibitions were, in 1779, in respect of boats to row with more than six oars, extended to all other English counties; the port of Bristol only excepted.

As for smuggling craft captured with smuggled goods the way of the revenue authorities with such was drastic. They were sawn up in three pieces, and then thoroughly broken up.

The futility of these extraordinary steps is emphasised by the report of the Commissioners of Customs to the Treasury in 1733, that immense smuggling operations were being conducted in Kent, Sussex, Essex, and Suffolk. In twelve months, this report declared, 54,000 lb. of tea and 123,000 gallons of brandy had been seized, and still, in spite of these tremendous losses, the spirit of the smugglers was unbroken, and smuggling was increasing. An

THE STRONG HAND 41

additional force of 106 Dragoons was asked for, to stiffen that of 185 already patrolling those coasts.

It was clearly required, with the utmost urgency, for such a mere handful of troops spread over this extended seaboard could scarce be considered a sufficient backing for the civil force, in view of the determined encounters continually taking place, in which the recklessness and daring of the smugglers knew no bounds. Thus, in June 1733, the officers of customs at Newhaven, attempting to seize ten horses laden with tea, at Cuckmere, were opposed by about thirty men, armed with pistols and blunderbusses, who fired on the officers, took them prisoners, and kept them under guard until the goods were safely carried off.

In August of the same year the riding-officers, observing upwards of twenty smugglers at Greenhay, most of them on horseback, pluckily essayed to do their duty and seize the goods, but the smugglers fell furiously upon them, and with clubs knocked one off his horse, severely wounded him, and confined him for an hour, while the run was completed. Of his companions no more is heard. They probably— to phrase it delicately—went for assistance.

In July 1735, customs officers of the port of Arundel, watching the coast, expecting goods to be run from a hovering smuggler craft, were discovered by a gang of more than twenty armed smugglers, anxiously waiting for the landing, and not disposed for an all-night trial of endurance in that waiting game. They accordingly seized the officers and confined them until some boat-loads of contraband had been landed and conveyed away on horseback. In the same month, at Kingston-by-the-Sea, between Brighton and Shoreham, some officers, primed with information of a forthcoming run of brandy, and seeking it, found as well ten smugglers with pistols. Although the smugglers were bold and menacing, the customs men on this occasion had the better of it, for they seized and duly impounded the brandy.

A more complicated affair took place on December 6th of the same year, when some customs officers of Newhaven met a large, well-armed gang of smugglers, who surrounded them and held them prisoners for an hour and a half. The same gang then fell in with another party, consisting of three riding-officers and six Dragoons, and were bold enough to attack them. Foolish enough, we must also add; for they got the worst of the encounter, and, fleeing in disorder, were pursued; five—armed with pistols, swords, and cutlasses, and provided with twelve horses—being captured.

A fatal encounter took place at Bulverhythe, between Hastings and Bexhill, in March 1737. It is best read of in the anonymous letter written to the Commissioners of Customs by a person who, for fear of the smuggling gangs, was afraid to disclose his real name, and subscribed himself " Goring." The letter—whose cold-blooded informing, the work evidently of an educated, but cruel-minded person, is calculated to make any reader of generous instincts shiver—is to be found among the customs correspondence, in the Treasury Papers.

" May it please [your] Honours,—It is not unknown to your Lordships of the late battle between the Smuglers and Officers at Bulverhide; and in relation to that Business, if your Honours but please to advise in the News Papers, that this is expected off, I will send a List of the names of the Persons

AN INFORMER

that were at that Business, and the places' names where they are usually and mostly resident. Cat (Morten's man) fired first, Morten was the second that fired; the soldiers fired and killed Collison, wounded Pigon, who is since dead; William Weston was wounded, but like to recover. Young Mr. Bowra was not there, but his men and horses were; from your Honours'

" Dutifull and Most faithfull servant,
" GORING.

" There was no foreign persons at this Business, but all were Sussex men, and may easily be spoke with.

" This [is] the seventh time Morten's people have workt this winter, and have not lost anything but one half-hundred [of tea] they gave to a Dragoon and one officer they met with the first of this winter; and the Hoo company have lost no goods, although they constantly work, and at home too, since they lost the seventy hundred-weight. When once the Smuglers are drove from home they will soon all be taken. Note, that some say it was Gurr that fired first. You must well secure Cat, or else your Honours will soon lose the man; the best way will be to send for him up to London, for he knows the whole Company, and hath been Morten's servant two years. There were several young Chaps with the Smuglers, whom, when taken, will soon discover the whole Company. The number was twenty-six men. Mack's horses, Morten's, and Hoak's, were killed, and they lost not half their goods. They have sent for more goods, and twenty-nine horses set out from Groombridge this day, about four in the afternoon, and all the men well armed with long guns.

"And if I hear this is received, I will send your Honours the Places names where your Honours will intercep the Smuglers as they go to Market with their Goods, but it must be done by Soldiers, for they go stronger now than ever. And as for Mr. Gabriel Tompkin, Supervisor of Dartford, there can be good reason given that Jacob Walter brought him Goods for three years last past, and it is likewise no dispute of that matter amongst allmost all the Smuglers. The Bruces and Jacob fought about that matter and parted Company's, and Mr. Tompkin was allway, as most people know, a villain when a Smugler and likewise Officer. He never was concern'd with any Body but Jacob, and now Jacob has certainly done with Smugling. I shall not trouble your Honours with any more Letters if I do not hear from this, and I do assure your Honours what I now write is truth.

"There are some Smuglers with a good sum of money, and they may pay for taking; as Thomas Darby, Edward King, John Mackdanie, and others that are rich.

"The Hoo Company might have been all ruined when they lost their goods; the Officers and Soldiers knew them all, but they were not prosecuted, as [they] was not at Groombridge, when some time since a Custom House Officer took some Tea and Arms too in Bowra's house at Groombridge.

"The first of this Winter, the Groombridge Smuglers were forced to carry their goods allmost all up to Rushmore Hill and Cester Mark, which some they do now, but Tea sells quick in London now, and Chaps from London come down to Groombridge almost every day, as they used to do last Winter. When once they come to be drove from

STERNER MEASURES

home, they will be put to great inconveniences, when they are from their friends and will lose more Goods than they do now, and be at more Charges. Do but take up some of the Servants, they will soon rout the Masters, for the Servants are all poor.

" Young Bowra's House cost £500 building, and he will pay for looking up.

" Morten and Bowra sold, last Winter, some-ways, about 3,000 [lb.] weight a week."

We hear nothing further of " Goring," and there is nothing to show who was the person whose cold malignance appears horribly in every line of his communication. Any action that may have been officially taken upon it is also hidden from us. But we may at least gather from it that the master-men, the employers of the actual smugglers of the goods, were in a considerable way of business, and already making very large profits. We see, too, that the smuggling industry was even then well on towards being a powerful organisation.

Still sterner legislative methods were, accordingly, in the opinion of the authorities, called for, and the Act of Indemnity of 1736 was the first result. This was a peculiarly mean and despicable measure, even for a Revenue Act. There is this excuse—although a small one—for it; that the Government was increasingly pressed for money, and that the enormous leakage to customs dues might possibly in some degree be lessened by stern and not very high-minded laws. By this Act it was provided that smugglers who desired (whether on trial or not) to obtain a free pardon for past offences, might do so by fully disclosing them; at the same time giving the names of their fellows. The especial iniquity of this lamentable example of frantic legislation, striking as it did at the very foundations of character in the creation of the informer and the sneak, is a sad instance of the moral obliquity to which a Government under stress of circumstances can descend.

The Act further proceeded to deal with backsliders who, having purged themselves as above, again resumed their evil courses, and it made the ways of transgressors very hard indeed; for, when captured, they were charged with not only their present offence, but also with that for which they had compounded with the Dev— that is to say, with the law. And, being so charged, and duly convicted, their case was desperate; for if the previous offence had carried with it, on conviction, a sentence of transportation (as many smuggling offences did : among them the carrying of firearms by three, or more men, while engaged in smuggling goods), the second brought a sentence of death.

With regard to the position of the pardoned smuggler who had earned his pardon by thus peaching on his fellows, it is not too much to say—certainly so far as the more ferocious smuggling gangs of Kent and Sussex were concerned—that by so doing he had already earned his capital sentence; for the temper of these men was such, and the risks they were made to run by these ferocious Acts were so great, that they would not—and, in a way of looking at these things, could not—suffer an informer to live.

Thus, even the additional inducements offered to informers by statute—including a reward of £50 each for the discovery and conviction of two or more accomplices—very generally failed to obtain results.

ULTIMATE PENALTIES

Many other items of unexampled severity were included in this Act, and in the yet more drastic measures of 1745 and the following year. By these it was provided that persons found loitering within five miles of the sea-coast, or any navigable river, might be considered suspicious persons; and they ran the risk of being taken before a magistrate, who was empowered, on any such person being unable to give a satisfactory account of himself, to commit him to the House of Correction, there to be whipped and kept at hard labour for any period not exceeding one month.

In 1746, assembling to run contraband goods was made a crime punishable with death as a felon, and counties were made liable for revenue losses. Smuggled goods seized and afterwards rescued entailed a fine of £200 upon the county; a revenue officer beaten by smugglers cost the county £40; or if killed, £100; with the provision that the county should be exempt if the offenders were convicted within six months.

As regards the offenders themselves, if they failed to surrender within forty days and were afterwards captured, the person who captured them was entitled to a reward of £500.

Dr. Johnson's definition of a smuggler appears on the title-page of the present volume. It is not a flattering testimonial to character; but, on the other hand, his opinion of a Commissioner of Excise—and such were the sworn enemies of smugglers—was much more unfavourable. Such an one was bracketed by the doctor with a political pamphleteer, or what he termed "a scribbler for a party," as one of "the two lowest of human beings." Without the context in which these judgments are now placed, it would be more than a little difficult to trace their reasoning, which sounds as little sensible as it would be to declare at one and the same time a burglar to be a dangerous pest and a policeman a useless ornament. But if smugglers can be proved from these pages wicked and reckless men, so undoubtedly shall we find the Commissioners of Excise and Customs, in their several spheres, appealing to the basest of human instincts, and thus abundantly worthy of Johnson's censure.

The shifts and expedients of the Commissioners of Customs for the suppression of smuggling were many and ingenious, and none was more calculated to perform the maximum of service to the Revenue with the minimum of cost than the commissioning of privateers, authorised to search for, to chase, and to capture if possible any smuggling craft. "Minimum of cost" is indeed not the right expression for use here, for the cost and risks to the customs establishment were *nil*. It should be said here that, although the Acts of Parliament directed against smuggling were of the utmost stringency, they were not always applied with all the severity possible to be used; and, on the other hand, customs officers and the commanders of revenue cutters were well advised to guard against any excess of zeal in carrying out their instructions. To chase and capture a vessel that every one knew perfectly well to be a smuggler, and then to find no contraband aboard, because, as a matter of fact, it had been carefully sunk at some point where it could easily be recovered at leisure, was not only not the way to promotion as a zealous officer; but was, on the contrary, in the absence of proof that contraband had been carried, a certain way to official disfavour.

And it was also, as many officers found to their cost, the way into actions at law, with resultant heavy damages not infrequently awarded against them. It was, indeed, a scandal that these public servants, who assuredly rarely ever brought to, or overhauled, a vessel without reasonable and probable cause, should have been subject to such contingencies, without remedy of any kind.

The happy idea of licensing private adventurers to build and equip vessels to make private war upon smuggling craft, and to capture them and their cargoes, was an extension of the original plan of issuing letters of marque to owners of vessels for the purpose of inflicting loss upon an enemy's commerce; but persons intending to engage upon this private warfare against smuggling had, in the first instance, to give security to the Commissioners of a diligence in the cause thus undertaken, and to enter into business details respecting the cargoes captured. It was, however, not infrequently found, in practice, that these privateers very often took to smuggling on their own account, and that, under the protective cloak of their ostensible affairs, they did a very excellent business; while, to complete this picture of failure, those privateers that really did keep to their licensed trade generally contrived to lose money and to land their owners into bankruptcy.

CHAPTER III

TERRORISING BANDS OF SMUGGLERS—THE HAWKHURST GANG—ORGANISED ATTACK ON GOUDHURST—THE " SMUGGLERS' SONG "

BUT the smugglers of Kent and Sussex were by far the most formidable of all the " free-traders " in England, and were not easily to be suppressed. Smuggling, export and import, off those coasts was naturally heavier than elsewhere, for there the Channel was narrower, and runs were more easily effected. The interests involved were consequently much greater, and the organisation of the smugglers, from the master-men to the labourers, was more nearly perfect. To interfere with any of the several confederacies into which these men were banded for the furtherance of their illicit trade was therefore a matter of considerable danger, and, well knowing the terror into which they had thrown the country-side, they presumed upon it, to extend their activities into other, and even less reputable, doings. The intervals between carrying tubs and otherwise working for the master-smugglers became filled, towards the middle of the eighteenth century, with acts of highway robbery and housebreaking, and, in the home counties, at any rate, smuggling proved often to be only the first step in a career of crime.

Among these powerful and terrorising confederacies, the Hawkhurst gang was pre-eminent.

A SMUGGLER'S WAREHOUSE 51

The constitution of it was, necessarily, a matter of inexact information, for the officers and the rank and file of such societies are mentioned by no minute-books or reports. But one of its principals was, without question, Arthur Gray, or Grey, who was one of those "Sea Cocks" after whom Seacox Heath, near Hawkhurst, in Kent, is supposed to be named. He was a man who did things on, for those times, a grand scale, and was said to be worth £10,000. He had built on that then lonely ridge of ground, overlooking at a great height the Weald of Kent, large store-houses—a kind of illicit "bonded warehouses"—for smuggled goods, and made the spot a distributing centre. That all these facts should have been contemporaneously known, and Gray's store not have been raided by the Revenue, points to an almost inconceivable state of lawlessness. The buildings were in after years known as "Gray's Folly"; but it was left for modern times to treat the spot in a truly sportive way: when Lord Goschen, who built the modern mansion of Seacox Heath on the site of the smuggler's place of business, became Chancellor of the Exchequer. If the unquiet ghosts of the old smugglers ever revisit their old haunts, how weird must have been the ironic laughter of Gray at finding this the home of the chief financial functionary of the Government!

In December 1744 the gang were responsible for the impudent abduction of a customs officer and three men who had attempted to seize a run of goods at Shoreham. They wounded the officer and carried the four off to Hawkhurst, where they tied two of them, who had formerly been smugglers and had ratted to the customs service, to trees, whipped them almost to death, and then took them down to the coast again and shipped them to France. A reward of £50 was offered, but never claimed.

To exhume yet another incident from the forgotten doings of the time : In March 1745 a band of twelve or fourteen smugglers assaulted three custom-house officers whom they found in an alehouse at Grinstead Green, wounded them in a barbarous manner, and robbed them of their watches and money.

In the same year a gang entered a farmhouse near Sheerness, in Sheppey, and stole a great quantity of wool, valued at £1,500. A week later £300 worth of wool, which may or may not have been a portion of that stolen, was seized upon a vessel engaged in smuggling it from Sheerness, and eight men were secured.

March 1746. A petition was forwarded to the House of Commons, entitled " An Humble Proposal to the Legislature for the effectual suppression of the most pernicious practice of Smuggling," wherein it was pointed out that " The method taken for many years by the Commissioners of Customs to whose care the Water Guard is committed has been to fit out armed vessels to cruise on the smugglers. But of late the smugglers have out-built them, and frequently bid them defiance. No provision is made for the men employed in the service, or their families, in case they are disabled or killed, nor is there any reward for apprehending at sea these worst as well as most desperate malefactors." Consequently, it was proposed, " Instead of burning the smuggling vessels as they now are, to be given with all their cargo to their captors : as also a reward the same as is given for the taking of

LOSS TO THE REVENUE

highwaymen, viz. £40 a head and recompense in case of loss of life or limb; but all upon this condition, that they suffer none to escape: it having been the practice for many years, if not by direct bribery, yet by a sort of tacit compromise to take only cargo and let the offenders go, which is almost become another illicit trade, and to which the growth of smuggling may principally be ascribed, as will plainly appear by comparing the vast quantities of goods taken at sea with the very small number of smugglers delivered up to Government." By a particular account of goods smuggled into the county of Suffolk between May 1745 and January 1746, it appears that great quantities of goods were run by several gangs of smugglers well armed from vessels which put into Benacre, Sizewell and other places, loaded on horses from 20 to 200 in a body. The total of them is 4,551; and supposing their loading to be one half tea and one half brandy, the loss to the revenue and nation by specie carried abroad will stand thus:

	Loss to the revenue.	Specie carried abroad.
2,275 horses loaded with tea at 1½ cwt. each, the neat pounds will be 382,144 lb.; at 2s. 6d. per lb. for customs and excise is . . .	£47,768	
and at 2s. per lb. for first cost abroad is		£38,214
2,276 horses loaded with brandy at 1½ cwt. each will be about 2s. per gallon per horse, making 47,796 gallons neat; at about 5s. a gallon for excise and customs is	£11,949	
and at 2s. a gallon for the first cost abroad is		£4,779
4,551 horses	£59,717	£42,993

In further proof of the enormous losses to the revenue caused by the smuggling trade, mention may be made of a pamphlet published two years earlier, entitled "A Proposal For Preventing Of Running Goods, etc." This was strongly recommended to the electors of Great Britain by most of the London papers. In it the writer stated that, "Since the excise duty of 4s. per lb. on tea was laid, it has brought an average of £130,000 a year into the Exchequer, which is but for 650,000 lb. weight of tea. But that the real consumption is vastly greater, a single fact will prove. Some years ago the Treasurer of our East India Coy. received a letter from Holland, intimating that one person in the Province of Zeeland smuggled yearly from England no less than half a million of pounds. Though this seemed incredible, the Directors, upon inquiry, were convinced of the fact that such a person there was, who some years before had been but an English sailor, was now married to a woman that kept a china shop, and had so well managed affairs that he had four sloops of his own constantly employed in smuggling, that the quantity of tea he was supposed to export had not at all been magnified, and that he had more guineas and English specie in his house than any banker in England." The remedy proposed by the author was that already alluded to, viz. a tax on all families drinking tea: "This will immediately hinder the running of any sorts of tea, the consumption of which is computed at 1,500,000 lb. a year, in Great Britain." He further incidentally alludes to "the multitudes of false oaths which are daily made at the Custom House, where they are grown so very familiar that a 'Custom-House Oath' has long ago passed into a proverb."

At about this time it was estimated by reliable

A TALE OF A PARSON   55

authorities that seven millions of pounds of tea was smuggled into the country annually : while the actual sales of the East India Company, which enjoyed a monopoly, amounted to under six million pounds.

As regards the above-mentioned " Proposal " (March 1746), wherein attention was called to the absence of compensation for loss of life or limb in conflict with smugglers, it may be of interest to mention that in 1780—thirty-four years afterwards—the Commissioners of Customs issued a general order to their officers, in which they stated that, as the smugglers had become so bold as to threaten to sink the revenue cruisers, and consequently the seamen would not engage with them, the Commissioners therefore allow an annuity of £10 a year to every mariner who should lose a hand or a foot. The loss of an eye was, apparently, considered of little account, no recompense being attached to it.

The following gives us a curious insight into contemporary manners and customs. The Supervisor at Canterbury writes in 1746 to Mr. Collier : " On the 7th inst. (March) a gang of about 150 smugglers landed their cargo between Reculver and Birchington and went from the sea-coast. Sixty-three men and 80 or 90 horses went by Whitstable and Faversham, and the rest over Grove Ferry. The Rev. Mr. Patten of Whitstable has let the Commissioners know when some gangs went through Whitstable for Faversham. It is reported he formerly received tythe from some smugglers, but these gangs being such ' rugged colts ' (as the Doct. calls them), that nothing is to be got from them made him angry."

A few days later we find General Henry Hawley

(the notorious General Hawley who was defeated so shamefully by the Pretender's followers at Falkirk the preceding year), writing to the Commissioners of Customs with regard to the distribution of the Royal Dragoons under his command, and asking for delay in the troops taking up their quarters—"till the roads in the East of Sussex are more passable for the partys to be able to move about."

And in June, Captain Gallantin, commanding the Dragoons stationed at Battle, reports to General Hawley: "If you intend that we should go to Maidstone or Tunbridge or Grinstead, it would be very proper to make the War Office send us a discretionary route, because they know nothing at all of the country, nor of the roads, that are worse than can be imagined by people who have not seen them." And he goes on to report the outbreak of distemper at Bexhill,—"which has been spread by the smugglers' horses and is carrying off great numbers of horses, which may render it necessary to remove the Dragoons."

On April 1st there was a large seizure of goods effected at Sandwich—"with the assistance of volunteers (15), who were recommended for a gratuity." The Superintendent writes of this affair: "Such a scene happened yesterday in Wingham street amongst ye smugglers, that I believe nothing like of ye sort has, since ye Creation. The smugglers, Mr. Cowper took part of ye goods from, entered into bond with the whole gang, that each party should stay at ye sea side till they were all loaded. But everyone got his load and shifted for himself as soon as possible. The last, and which lost their goods, were some Sussex, Hawkhurst, and Folkestone, &c. The whole cargo, it's reported, was

EXTENSIVE SEIZURES

$11\frac{1}{2}$ ton of Tea, &c., and 350 horses employed. The Sussex and Hawkhurst men, resenting the others leaving them (as is supposed), went home, and forthwith 92 men returned with fuzees, pistols and Broad swords. It is thought some of them were concerned in another boat that Capt. Martin took yesterday morning with $9\frac{1}{2}$–$7\frac{1}{2}$ ton of Tea, it is said. The above 92 men intended to have took the goods of those that left ye coast before the rest and rescued the goods at Margate. They were together yesterday morning at Wingham, where they fight with swords, &c.; 7 men were wounded and 2 very much. At last Sussex and Hawkhurst were masters of ye field and carried off 40 horses belonging to Folkestone, &c. The dogs were so attrociously inclined that some inhabitants belonging to Wingham went to the outparts thereof to prevent travellers going through. Any horseman they (the smugglers) saw was conducted by some, sword in hand, to ye main army, where the prisoner left his horse. They at last went to Waldershire, but where now I have not heard. I fancy this affair will demolish many of them, and in truth, if they are not, the time will come when few will accept of places in ye Customs where their duty requires riding."

Mr. Collier, in his reply says: " I joyne with you in the opinion that this affair may be attended with service and in good probability make them desperate and discovery obtainable."

The following extracts from a correspondence between the Prime Minister, Mr. Pelham and Mr. Collier, in 1746, are not without significance. Under date May 23rd, 1746, Mr. Pelham writes: " I have great complaints of the violence and increasing of smuggling in our country, which tho' you know I have always been an enemy to, and given no protection to any persons concerned in it, yet great reproaches are thrown out upon me, and calumny, tho' undeserved, will have its effect. They tell me there are regular boats going between Hastings and Bullogne, not only upon smuggling affairs but also carrying on very improper correspondencys."

To this Mr. Collier replies, under date May 29th: "There are companies of soldiers quartered along the coast to assist Magistrates," and after denying any improper correspondence with Boulogne, he adds, "during the late threatened invasion and descent from France, no boats from Hastings were in French ports between 1st Dec. and April: nor were any boats in Holland, Guernsey or Jersy on smuggling practices." And he goes on to refer to the pamphlet of Admiral Vernon, called "Seasonable Advice," in which it was insinuated that he (Mr. Collier) encouraged the smugglers, which he indignantly denies.

The following from Mr. Collier to Admiral Vernon, dated December 14th, 1746, has reference to the threatened attempt to invade England: "Sir, the 9th inst. I had intelligence that there were fitting out with the utmost expedition, at Boulogne, all their privateers, trading ships and fishing boats, and all prizes in the harbour taken from us in this war, and cleansing the Slub out of their harbour, or basin, that they might ride or float, and that it was publicly talked of that they were designed to bring over soldiers to be landed on the Coast of Kent or Sussex and were to be ready in Ten days. . . . On the 14th inst. at 3 in the morning I had a letter from his Grace the Duke of Newcastle that his Majesty

MILITARY REPRESSION

had received certain intelligence preparations were making at Dunkirk and other parts of France for making an immediate descent upon some parts of the Coast: and that intelligence of any vessels appearing off the coast was to be sent to his Grace and to Admiral Vernon in the Downs."

It is recorded that in May 1746 "Two brigades were ordered to the Coasts of Sussex to awe the smugglers,"—with what result the sequel will show.

January 1747. Several vessels are reported loading with cargoes of tea for the Sussex coast.

The following correspondenee refers to a man called Wyman who had turned informer and given evidence on behalf of the Crown at the trials of two smugglers, Fuller and Austin. The Supervisor at Hythe writes to Mr. Collier: " (Feb. 8th, 1747) At his return home from your house the last time he was there he was laid in wait for by some smugglers, but fortunately passed them unknown, as he has since been informed. He complains of being badly treated by Mr. Polhill (Riding Officer) of Lydd, who, when he came to Ashford, went into the company with Brooks and other Proclaimed Smugglers from Hawkhurst, told them what he had been about himself and that Wyman was an evidence for the King, so that his house, though a mile from Ashford, is besett 2 or 3 nights in a week, and he threatened to be murdered if they can meet with him." And he goes on to state that he (the writer) gave Wyman 5s. subsistence " to encourage him," and adds: " As to the truth of what he charges Polhill with, he has signed a certificate with his own hand to certify it. I am sorry any officer under my inspection should be guilty of betraying his trust. I know what such a one deserves; but I will say no more." He encloses Wyman's certificate, which runs as follows: "These are to certify that I William Wyman have been betrayed to the smugglers Proclaimed, in that I have been evidence for the King against some, and that I dare not keep my house, because severall smugglers have besett it, and swear they wil murder me. I am betrayed by Mr. Polhill, Rideing officer in the Customs at Lydd." Together with the certificate, Wyman forwards a letter received from Cranbrook: "Sir, Having lately heard that you have something against Tho. Potter of Benenden, a noted smuggler, for which you are willing to prosecute him, I send you this to inform you that he was taken about a month ago, and is now in Maidstone gaol: and as it is most likely that he will be tried at the next Assizes, I hope your regard for your own safety, and your love to your country, will not suffer you to delay in a matter of so great importance, but use your utmost endeavour to bring him and all such villains to justice. I and many of my neighbours are threatened with death, but we are resolved by the blessing of God upon our endeavour to rid the country of them. And this I hope and trust is your mind also, in which I heartily wish you may continue and be successfull, and so remain your humble servant Wm. Skinner."

Mr. Collier, returned a vague and chilling reply to this strange communication, merely observing that, "he could give no advice about Goudhurst," and that the witness, Wyman, was to have "no money on his account." But writing some months later to Mr. Senior, in London, he says: "The smugglers have certainly used Wyman barbarously, drove him from place to place, and publicly declared they would murder him on any opportunity."

Thomas Potter, the man referred to above, was concerned with three others in rescuing William Gray, Kemp, and other smugglers from Newgate. This they effected in the following manner. They visited Gray and the others in the press-yard of Newgate, when they agreed at all hazards to assist in getting them out, and the time was then fixed on. On the day appointed the three men came together to the press-yard door, rang the bell for the turnkey to come and let them in, and on his opening the door, Potter immediately knocked him down with a horse-pistol and cut him terribly. Kemp and Gray then made their escape; the former had no irons on, but Gray had so arranged his irons as to let them fall off when he pleased. Three other prisoners got away at the same time, but having their irons on they were soon recaptured.

Potter was eventually arrested and tried at Rochester Assizes for divers robberies, and in particular for stealing a horse. He and three others who were tried along with him used to go in disguise and break into houses after dark, binding all the family, and then robbing. Potter was born at Hawkhurst and was twenty-eight years old, and confessed, before he was executed, that he had been guilty of all manner of crimes except murder; though he declared that he did design to murder the turnkey at Newgate when he went to get Gray and Kemp out; but he was glad it was no worse than happened, and he often prayed the man might recover of his wound; and when he heard that he was well again he was very glad. He further acknowledged that he had committed crimes sufficient to have hanged him for many years past, but solemnly declared that he knew nothing of the robbery for which he was to suffer, and he took the sacrament just before his execution, which took place on Penenden Heath, on March 30th, 1749, along with six others.

On April 6th, an informer named Darby, who had been badly maltreated, but, being still alive, would seem to have had a charmed life, writes to the Supervisor: "When I was at London you desired I would exert myself and procure affidavits against some of ye gang of smugglers that run on the coast the 7th inst. I have done all that is in my power to induce the person that informed me, but he is a farmer and lives at Reculver, and he says that he is afraid ye gang will burn down his house and barn if he should discover any of them, and so says everyone that I have interceeded with on this afear (affair), and they all say that as there is no Force in ye County, the smugglers will do as they please with them if they affront them."

During May a party of the Lifeguards set out for Kent to bring some smugglers up to London. Two smugglers named "Slip-jibbet" and "Tom-tit" were tried at Newgate; and seven others broke out, with pistols and bludgeons, but were retaken. There is frequent mention in the public Press at this time of "Gray the smuggler who broke out of Newgate."

In June we read that all H.M. ships that could be got ready for sea are ordered to cruise in the Channel, as several smuggling cutters are reported loading in the French ports. Also, the Commissioners of Customs write to Mr. Collier: "Having received information that the smugglers from Rye

OUTRAGES BY SMUGGLERS

and Hastings have carried to France 60 or 70 swivel guns and that they openly carry over wool, the inhabitants not daring to stop them, I desire you will make enquiry, &c., and give your opinion how it may be prevented."

In July comes word that two smugglers went to an alehouse, and, not being admitted quickly enough, smashed in the door, shot the landlord in the leg and then beat him brutally. The smugglers were at length seized, but one escaping brought back a gang of thirty armed with cutlasses and pistols, who proceeded to attack the house of a large farmer near, whose servants were supposed to have helped to secure their mate. They pulled his wife—who was near her time—out of bed, and made her tell where the cash was, and took forty guineas and all the plate they could find: they then smashed everything in the house, staved all the beer and ale barrels, drunk all the wine and brandy, and then rode off in triumph through the town, defying everyone. The farmer's loss was about £300.

At the same time came news that a party of outlawed smugglers were riding about the country in the neighbourhood of Croydon, in carters' smocks, well mounted, and were robbing everyone: they even robbed some poor reapers of their money. Also came news that "Blood-thirsty," a smuggler, is seized near Maidstone by a party of soldiers after a desperate resistance.

Also came news that four soldiers had been shot by the smugglers, who threaten the printers for publishing advertisements against them.

In September Thomas Puryour, alias "Black Tooth," smuggler, was sentenced to death at the Old Bailey. Also five smugglers brought from

Folkestone were ordered to remain till next session. Also one Austin a smuggler taken at Maidstone was committed; he was taken with great difficulty, being armed, and he killed a sergeant.

On October 7th sixty armed smugglers broke open the custom house at Poole and carried away upwards of 4,000 lb. weight of tea lately seized by the *Swift*, Privateer.

On the 27th Mr. Collier writes to the Solicitor to the Customs: " The Cranbrook Association (probably volunteers like Goodhurst Militia) last week apprehended Wm. Gray of Hawkhurst, one of that gang of smugglers who have so many years triumphed over the officers of the Revenue and struck terror into the country for so many years. He was carried before a Justice of the Peace, but as he is none of the proscribed persons, nor anything particular against him, he was discharged, on which I hear he has become more insolent than ever, as he has been one of the most notorious Fellows and concerned in running many thousand pounds of goods. He has lately built a house at Goudhurst which is thought to have cost at least £1,200 or £1,500. All I ever heard in his favour is that he showed some humanity and compassion to the officers apprehended at Shoreham in Kent, but is said to be one of the contrivers of that villany. Tripp, alias Stanford, is another head of the Hawkhurst gang and has built a house costing about £700, and is one of the persons that stands indicted for the murder of Carswell of this place (Hastings) and has never been apprehended; indeed the smugglers either bought off the chief evidence, or else murdered him, so that there is not sufficient for conviction. I believe there may be also materials in

THE HAWKHURST GANG

Mr. Metcalfe's office to secure him. This will be a striking deadly blow and entirely destroy this nest of vermin : and now the affair is on the anvil, and carried on hitherto with success, I hope it will be continued. These persons, as I am informed, pretend to have intelligence if anything is taken out against them, and keep a person in perpetual pay for that purpose, so that there must be the greatest secrecy, and persons to take them must be sent from London. I hint this, but desire my name in regard to Wm. Gray and Tripp, alias Stanford, may not be made use of, nor known but only to yourself."

We read at this time of great numbers of robberies by outlawed smugglers; several of whom had already been captured and executed; as, for example, Richard Ashcraft—" the first smuggler convicted under the late Act." The officers and soldiers concerned in his capture received a reward of £500. Also, a corporal and two Dragoons who captured John Cook, lately executed, received £500.

The long immunity of the Hawkhurst gang from serious interference inevitably led to its operations being extended in every direction, and the law-abiding populace of Kent and Sussex eventually found themselves dominated by a great number of fearless marauders, whose will for a time was a greater law than the law of the land. None could take legal action against them without going hourly in personal danger, or in fear of house, crops, wheatstacks, hay-ricks, or stock being burnt or otherwise injured.

The village of Goudhurst, a picturesque spot situated upon a hill on the borders of Kent and Sussex, was the first place to resent this ignoble subserviency. The villagers and the farmers round about were wearied of having their horses commandeered by mysterious strangers for the carrying of contraband goods that did not concern them, and were determined no longer to have their houses raided with violence for money or anything else that took the fancy of these fellows.

They had at last found themselves faced with the alternatives, almost incredible in a civilised country, of either deserting their houses and leaving their property at the mercy of these marauders, or of uniting to oppose by force their lawless inroads. The second alternative was chosen; a paper expressive of their abhorrence of the conduct of the smugglers, and of the determination to oppose them, was drawn up and subscribed to by a considerable number of persons, who assumed the style of the "Goudhurst Band of Militia." At their head was a young man named Sturt, who had recently been a soldier. He it was who had persuaded the villagers to be men, and make some spirited resistance.

News of this unexpected stand on the part of these hitherto meek-spirited people soon reached the ears of the dreaded Hawkhurst gang, who contrived to waylay one of the "Militia," and, by means of torture and imprisonment, extorted from him a full disclosure of the plans and intentions of his colleagues. They swore the man not to take up arms against them, and then let him go; telling him to inform the Goudhurst people that they would, on a certain day named, attack the place, murder everyone in it, and then burn it to the ground.

Sturt, on receiving this impudent message,

GOUDHURST CHURCH

THE GOUDHURST AFFAIR   67

assembled his "Militia," and, pointing out to them the danger of the situation, employed them in earnest preparations. While some were sent to collect firearms, others were set to casting bullets and making cartridges, and to providing defences.

Punctually at the time appointed (a piece of very bad policy on their part, by which they would appear to have been fools as well as rogues) the gang appeared, headed by Thomas Kingsmill, and fired a volley into the village, over the entrenchments made. The embattled villagers replied, some from the houses and roof-tops, and others from the leads of the church-tower; when George Kingsmill, brother of the leading spirit in the attack, was shot dead. He is alluded to in contemporary accounts as the person who had killed a man at Hurst Green, a few miles distant.

In the firing that for some time continued two others of the smugglers, one Barnet Wollit and a man whose name is not mentioned, were killed and several wounded. The rest then fled, pursued by the valorous "Militia," who took a few prisoners, afterwards handed over by them to the law, and executed.

Surprisingly little is heard of this—as we, in these more equable times, are prone to think it—extraordinary incident. A stray paragraph or so in the chronicles of the time is met with, and that is all. It was only one of the usual lawless doings of the age.

But to-day the stranger in the village may chance, if he inquires a little into the history of the place, to hear wild and whirling accounts of this famous event; and, if he be at all enterprising, will find in the parish registers of burials this one piece of documentary evidence toward the execution done that day :

"1747, Ap. 20, George Kingsmill, Dux sclerum glande plumbeo emisso, cecidit."

All these things, moreover, are duly enshrined, amid much fiction, in the pages of G. P. R. James's novel, *The Smuggler*.

And still the story of outrage continued. On August 14th, 1747, a band of twenty swaggering smugglers rode, well-armed and reckless, into Rye and halted at the "Red Lion" inn, where they remained drinking until they grew rowdy and violent.

Coming into the street again, they discharged their pistols at random, and, as the old account of these things concludes, "observing James Marshall, a young man, too curious of their behaviour, carried him off, and he has not since been heard of."

History tells us nothing of the fate of that unfortunate young man; but, from other accounts of the bloodthirsty characters of these Kentish and Sussex malefactors, we imagine the very worst.

Others, contemporary with them—if, indeed, they were not the same men, as seems abundantly possible—captured two revenue officers near Seaford, and, securely pinning them down to the beach at low-water mark, so that they could not move, left them there, so that, when the tide rose, they were drowned.

Again, on September 14th of this same year, 1747, a smuggler named Austin, violently resisting arrest, shot a sergeant dead with a blunderbuss at Maidstone.

In "The Smugglers' Song " Mr. Rudyard Kipling has vividly reconstructed those old times of dread,

"THE GENTLEMEN GO BY"

'THE GENTLEMEN GO BY' 69

when, night and day, the numerous and well-armed bodies of smugglers openly traversed the country, terrorising everyone. To look too curiously at these high-handed ruffians was, as we have already seen, an offence, and the most cautious among the rustics made quite sure of not incurring their high displeasure—and incidentally of not being called upon by the revenue authorities as witnesses to the identity of any among their number—by turning their faces the other way when the free-traders passed. Mothers, too, were careful to bid their little ones on the Marshland roads, or in the very streets of New Romney, to turn their faces to the hedge-side, or to the wall, " when the gentlemen went by." And—

If you wake at midnight, and hear a horse's feet,
Don't go drawing back the blind, or looking in the street;
Them that ask no questions isn't told a lie,
Watch the wall, my darling, while the gentlemen go by.

   Five-and-twenty ponies
   Trotting through the dark—
   Brandy for the parson;
   'Baccy for the clerk;
   Laces for a lady; letters for a spy,
And watch the wall, my darling, while the gentlemen go by.

On November 17th, 1747, the gaol at Maidstone was broken open about eight in the evening by twelve persons armed and disguised, who wounded the keeper and his assistants and rescued Samuel Prior, Richard Blundell, Francis Marketman, and John Hales, notorious smugglers, and carried them to a place a little distant where a gang of at least twenty with horses were in readiness and conveyed them away. Another smuggler, James Holt, was violently rescued from the custody of some riding-officers.

On November 21st the Solicitor to the Customs writes, in a satirical vein to Mr. Collier: " As to Wm. Gray and Tripp, they are two gentlemen to whom the Revenue is greatly obliged, and if we could gett at them, so as to make them a suitable return for all their favours, it would be of great service." And a few days later, writing about the approaching trials of Samuel Austin, Thomas Kemp (one of the Hawkhurst gang), Peter Tickman, and James Hodges, alias " Poison," the Solicitor asks Mr. Collier to procure further evidence, adding that " Arthur Gray, who is in custody also, cannot be tried for want of evidence : he is reputed to be worth £10,000."

On December 12th the Solicitor writes again to Mr. Collier, concerning the trial of the above smugglers : " On Thursday, about 3 p.m., Wills was brought to me at the Old Bailey, but he was so drunk that we could not proceed that day. Yesterday we began with ye persons called Rough Ticknor and Poison. They were indicted for an offence in 1744, at Lydd Lights, which was introduced by a long account by John Baltern of his being surprised at Shoreham with two other officers, being carried from thence prisoners to Hawkhurst, being whipped and abused there in the most unmerciful manner, being carried from thence to the sea coast, confined there in chains, being forced to assist the smugglers in working their goods at Lydd Lights, and of the smugglers endeavouring to have transported him to Boulogne by the boat which brought the goods from thence. We had a second witness who saw the two prisoners with a part of this cargo in their way to London. Ye prisoners called no witnesses, except Mr. Masters, who spoke to the character of Poison.

TERRORISM

Ye Jury found them both guilty, and Ticknor went from the Barr shaking his fist at ye witnesses for the Crown. Ye publishing this extraordinary account in this manner to the City of London had its immediate use, and I hope will have its use even hereafter. The Court was more thronged than ever I yett saw it. Austin and Poison was also convicted after a long trial in which a boy (step-son) denied his own mother, but at last broke down under cross-examination and was convicted of purgury."

The difficulty of getting witnesses to come forward on behalf of the Crown, in these trials, is emphasised in a letter from the Superintendent at Canterbury to Mr. Collier: " The last time Mr. Senior sent to me to order the fellow (a witness) to London, I believe he did not go; when he parted from me, he promised me, and set out immediately: he was then almost dead with fear, expecting to be killed on the road, having been shot at and his horse wounded, and now lives a most shocking life: and those privy to his going up may be in danger if it is known. It was blowed in London he had sworn against the smugglers." And in special allusion to the Kentish coast, he adds : " the smugglers in those parts are got to as great a height as the Hawkhurst gang and have not been so much quelled."

The following, from Mr. Senior to Mr. Collier concerning the recent trials, helps to complete the picture of the times : " Ye person who is Sollicitor for the Smugglers when in Newgate is one Kelly, an Irish Roman Catholick. He has the assurance from his country, and his principles from his religion, or from Hell itself: and to make a gentleman so accomplished compleately a man of business, he has 40 or 50 fellows of his own country and religion at his command who are ever ready to swear whatever he cares to dictate." And the writer adds: "ye preparations which were made on Wednesday morning for the escape of Austin and Kempe terrified the keepers and alarmed the Court."

Again, on December 18th, Mr. Senior writes: "Arthur Gray stands convicted for robbery upon the highway in Kent, and for which he can only be tried in that county. I have not the least scrap of evidence against that fellow, except ye man has been very barbarous, outrageous and assiduous in smuggling with fire-arms, and is become extremely formidable and obnoxious to the Counties of Kent and Sussex. I think, therefore, that such a man would very deservedly suffer at Tyburn, and that if evidence could be had to convict him capitally as a smuggler, and to bring him to receive his punishment there, that it would be a great service to the community."

Mr. Collier, writing (December 31st, 1747) in reply to a request for information concerning a gang which ran goods at Eastbourne, states: "I have been with the Customs officer at Eastbourne and discoursed there in general terms about smuggling, and in particular of the gang of smugglers where Ashcraft was present and for which he suffered, and as it was in the day-time they must know a great many of them. Nothing came out relating to Arthur Gray or Thomas Kemp: on which the discourse rolled on the smugglers that have been executed, and those now in Newgate, and in particular of Arthur Gray, and I asked them about him, but could obtain no sort of evidence, only that it was universally looked upon that he was one of the most desperate of the gang. Other officers also said they had seen him

"TURNING THEIR FACES TO THE WALL"

and knew him, but never armed at the coast. It's very much that this fellow, one of the first of the Hawkhurst gang, has been for so many years publick in smuggling practices and been guilty of more acts of violence and barbarity and public vice than any of them, should escape going up Holborn Hill for want of evidence. He stands indicted at this Assize for the murder of Mr. Carswell a Customs officer of this place (Hastings) in 1744, on which he was apprehended; but he and the rest of the gang either bought off or destroyed the chief witness, that he could not be tried and consequently was bailed at the Assizes. He has by common fame robbed several persons on the highway in Kent, and has robbed a Laceman of goods to a considerable amount at Hawkhurst and barbarously cut and mangled one Lyon a Pedlar at the same place. There is hardly any villainy he has not been guilty of, and so desperate a fellow, that the country have trembled at his name, and I believe his being taken off will be more satisfaction than almost any other two."

December 31st, Mr. Collier receives the following important intelligence from the custom-house, London: " We have it in ye news, of one Gray's being taken, a noted smuggler. Should be glad to hear it to be ye noted Will Gray of Hawkhurst, Cooke's master and of whom he so bitterly complains in his dyeing speech."

With regard to the notorious smuggler, Arthur Gray, whose villainies have been alluded to, we find the Supervisor at Hythe writing to Mr. Collier, under date February 19th, 1748 : " I beg to enclose the examination of one John Pelham who deposed to having seen the notorious Arthur Gray on 13th Aug., 1746, working a boat loaded with tea and brandy, and that he was armed at the time, and that he had seen him come into Lydd, armed with fire-arms, in a riotous manner." And next day Mr. Polhill, the officer at Lydd, reports having obtained another evidence against Arthur Gray. And on the 27th Mr. Senior writes from London to Mr. Collier, informing him that on the evidence obtained (as above) he had indicted Arthur and William Gray. As regards the latter, he adds : " I find many are to appear for him, and (what I am sure you will think very strange) many are Custom House officers."

March 1748, news came that Mr. Springer, an officer of the customs in Sussex, was carried away by a gang of smugglers and put on board a vessel near Brighthelmstone to be sent to France. Also that two persons who were going to be evidence for the King against the rioters at Poole are missing, supposed to be killed. (This refers to the barbarous murders of Galley, a customs officer, and Chater, a witness for the Crown, as detailed in Chapter IV., while on their way to Major Battine, a Justice of the Peace for that county.)

From the following letter, dated April 5th, it would seem that the smugglers could reckon on connivance with their outrages in very high quarters. Mr. Senior writes Mr. Collier : " Anyone would think that a country so harassed as the county of Sussex has been by these ruffians should think of them when they see them at the Barr, as Mr. St. John declared himself upon the Bill for attainting Lord Stafford, and not acquit them in violation of the law and their oath to give a true verdict according to the evidence. But may this man's (Carne) acquittal be upon them and upon their children. If the Government be at last obliged to exterminate these creatures by the sword, these instances will justify such a procedure." And he goes on to mention the escape of William Gray from the prison, under the supposed acquiescence of the jailer; and how both Gray and Kemp (who escaped same time) were seen drinking at a public house at Battle at the very time when some of the townspeople were inside reading the advertisement for their apprehension.

The next is from Mr. Polhill, officer at Hythe, to Mr. Collier informing him of Arthur Gray's conviction on the evidence of himself and two others: adding, "there is three more smugglers yt to be try'd, but are this morning taken with the smallpox." Next day (April 23rd) came a letter from Mr. Senior to Mr. Collier confirming the above: " He (Arthur Gray) was convicted capitally yesterday. He had one friend on the Jury most certainly. But upon the whole it would not do. Ye taking off so brutal a creature I hope will be attended with good consequences."

The man Thomas Kemp, who escaped from Newgate along with William Gray, had been already recaptured; and although not again mentioned in this correspondence, his career deserves to be noticed. He and his brother, Lawrence Kemp, were both born near Hawkhurst, had been smugglers for many years, and both belonged to the Hawkhurst gang. Thomas Kemp, at the time of his escape from Newgate, was confined on a charge of debt to the Crown. The charge on which both brothers were tried at the Chichester Assizes, on January 18th, 1749, and received sentence of death, was for robbing the house of a farmer called Hevendon of Heathfield, Kent, the previous November. According to the evidence of Hevendon, at about seven in the evening, he heard somebody whistle at his door, and going out to see who was there, four men with crape over their faces seized him, put a pistol to his breast, and said they wanted money; upon which he gave them 11s. 6d. out of his pocket, but they said that would not do, and took him into the house, called for candles, and one of them holding a pistol to his breast, stayed with him, while the rest went upstairs, and after some time, returned with what they had got. They then took him to the place where they had left their horses, and swore they would carry him off unless he told them where the rest of his money was; but when they were got on their horses, they bid him good-night, and left him. When he got back to his house, he found they had broken open two doors, two trunks, and a box, and had carried away thirty-five pounds in money, two silver spoons, three gold rings, a silver cup, and a silver watch in a tortoiseshell case.

The manner of their arrest was singular, and was effected, accidentally, so to say, through the agency of an outlawed smuggler, one William Pring, who, in order to obtain pardon and his freedom, turned informer, and made an offer to arrest John Mills, one of the ruffians wanted in connection with the murder of Galley and Chater. Pring's offer was accepted, and his pardon promised; so he set off for Bristol, where he knew Mills had gone to sell some smuggled goods; and there, unexpectedly, met with the Kemps, both of whom he knew were wanted; one for breaking out of Newgate; the other, Lawrence, being outlawed by proclamation. Mills being with them, Pring laid a snare for entrapping all three. To this end he advised them, as they were all alike in desperate circumstances, to go along with him to his house at Beckenham in Kent, where they would form a plan to go robbing upon the highway, and break open houses, in the same way as " Gregory's gang " used to do. This being agreed on, they all went to his house at Beckenham, where, on arrival, Pring, pretending that the horse he had with him was a bad one, said he would go to London and fetch his mare, which was a good one, and be back as quickly as possible, when they would all set out together to rob. The others agreed to wait in his house till he returned. But Pring, instead of going to town, rode with all speed for Horsham, where he applied to the Excise officer for assistance, and accompanied by the officer and eight others, well armed, set out for Beckenham, which they reached in the middle of the night, and there they found Mills and the two Kemps just sitting down to supper upon a fine breast of veal. The two Kemps were quickly secured, but Mills being very refractory had to be cut down before he would submit to be bound.

Before their execution, the two Kemps declared that for two years past they had no "steady," meaning no fixed place of abode; and also, that if they had not been obliged to hide themselves, for fear of being taken up as smugglers, they would never have committed the robberies. They were executed near Horsham, on April 1st, without making any confessions, though they appealed to the spectators to take warning by their untimely end.

April 2nd. Thirty smugglers, armed with blunderbusses and pistols, following the example of those who broke open the custom house at Poole, last October, broke open the King's warehouse at Colchester at two in the morning, with a blacksmith's hammer and crow, and carried off sixty oil bags containing about 1,514 lb. of tea.

May 2nd, 1748, comes confirmation of the news of the recapture of William Gray : " I am glad to hear Gray is once more in Hold," writes the Solicitor to Mr. Collier, "and hope he'll soon take a trip and join his brother Arthur upon the same Gibbett." And on the 31st he compliments the Surveyor-General on " the zeal with which you have acted, not to mention the dangers to which you have been exposed in some late services performed by you against the smugglers." On June 22nd comes news that William Gray is sentenced to seven years' transportation.

Under date June 6th the Collector of Land Taxes writes to Mr. Collier from Battle : " Sir, last night a person was sent to inform me of a design carrying on by a large gang of smugglers to take our cash and bills before my return to Petworth on Tuesday morning at 6 o'clock. I receive at Bourn, and in the afternoon from thence to Lewes, having about £10,000 in cash besides bills; " and he goes on to request the protection of a guard of soldiers.

On the same day Mr. Collier receives the following from his London agent : " If we have peace fixed, then sure you'll have enough soldiers to spare to pick up all the £500 chaps : for as they can be but hanged, let them do what mischief they will, so I doubt they'll do a deal before the Nubbing post (gallows) is their portion." And again, on the 25th June : " The smugglers, you'll perceive by this Dyeing speech, as well as all the former, are quite out of Luck. To be Tuck'd up and *all* innocent, not *one* guilty is cruell ffate. But they've the misfortun not to be left, and hanging still goes

MR. COLLIER

forward, so 'tis to be hoped 'twill to the end of the chapter." And again, on July 19th : " I had yesterday the good luck to meet with Mr. Ackerman (ye Governor of Newgate), who told me that he was very willing and ready to pay the £50 Reward for taking Gray, when he was satisfied who the persons were that were entitled to it." (See letter of May 2nd.) And in a subsequent letter he writes : " I've got Ackerman's £50 this day : " and later, " I also received the £100, at the Custom House, for the apprehending Gray."

Under date June 7th, 1748, Mr. Collier writes to a Mr. P. : " It is certain that Curtis, alias Pollard, and some of the Proclaimed smugglers are lurking about this part of the country. . . . The smugglers and their emissaries hover about the Custom House and have sometimes surprising intelligence of what is contained in publick letters, that it is feared some clerk is in with them."

The following letter apparently refers to one of the Chichester smugglers who was concerned in the flogging of a man to death under circumstances of revolting barbarity in a public-house on Slindon Common, Sussex (January 1748). The Solicitor to the Customs in London writes to Mr. Collier, under date June 16th, 1748, reporting that Jeremiah Curtis who had escaped from Newgate was in the neighbourhood of Hastings, and that officers had been sent to arrest him; and requesting Mr. Collier to render all the assistance in his power. Whereupon Mr. Collier replies : " The sending of two persons from London, strangers to this country and afraid to stir without a military assistance, I am afraid will not answer the intention."

Jeremiah Curtis, alias Pollard, alias Butler, one of

the worst of the ruffianly Hawkhurst gang, was wanted, along with John Mills, alias Smoker, for the murder of Richard Hawkins, a farm labourer of Yapton, on January 28th, 1748, in a manner which was described by Counsel for the Crown as "one of the most cruel and bloody murders that was ever perpetrated in this, or any other civilised country." They seized this poor fellow on suspicion of having stolen two bags of smuggled tea, carried him away to the "Dog and Partridge" Inn, at Slindon Common, where they flogged him with horse-whips and kicked him till he was dead; and they had actually set off to fetch the man's father and brother, in order to treat them in the same manner, when they were persuaded to turn back. They then carried the dead body by night to Parham Park, twelve miles off, where, after tying stones to it, they cast it into a pond belonging to Sir Cecil Bishop. Curtis escaped to France, and the last heard of him was that he had entered himself in the Corps of the Irish Brigades, at Gravelines.

His accomplice, John Mills, was trapped along with the two Kemps, as already described, at Beckenham. He was tried at the Chichester Assizes, in January 1749, and condemned to death. Previous to his execution he blamed Curtis for having been the principal person who drew him away from his honest employment as a colt-breaker at Trotton, near Liss. He also blamed the two witnesses for the Crown, on whose evidence he was convicted, for having broken the solemn oath they had sworn amongst themselves, and he "therefore wished that they might all come to the same end and be hanged like him, and be d——d afterwards." This wretch had committed two horrible murders within twenty days of each

INTIMIDATED SUSSEX

other He was executed near the "Dog and Partridge," and afterwards hung in chains there. His father and brother were convicted at the same Assizes for the murder of Galley and Chater, and hanged at Chichester.

The state of terrorism in which the inhabitants of Sussex were living at this time is graphically described by a gentleman writing from Horsham, under date August 23rd, 1748 : " Sir, I have frequently conversed with many gentlemen of fortune about these dangerous men, and they assure me that *the outlawed and other smugglers*, in this and the neighbouring counties, are so numerous and desperate that the inhabitants are in continual dread of the mischiefs which these horrid wretches not only threaten, but actually perpetrate all round the country. The outrageous proceedings which you see in the public papers are not a tithe of what they really commit, and to be quite familiar with you I cannot better describe the terror which they strike than by quoting Milton :

" ' O ! what are these,
Death's ministers, not men, who thus deal death
Inhumanly to men, and multiply
Ten thousand-fold the sin of him who slew
His brother; for of whom such massacre make they
But of their brethren, men of men ? ' "

Under the heading " The Cause of the Decay of Trade," the following noteworthy remarks will be found, under date September 3rd, 1748, in the *Remembrancer :* " The evil of smuggling arises wholly from high duties. It is universally counselled that lowering those high duties which first made smuggling a trade, would not only abolish it, but increase the revenue by increasing the consumption of the commodity so over-rated. Everybody is of opinion that there is no way so effectual to remove it as to remove the temptation. And everybody wonders that the same force which has been employed with so much success against the rebels of Scotland has not been more successfully employed against the rebels of Sussex. But these high duties are not enforced at the outports as they are in London. There is a species of importers in many of these places who are little better than licensed smugglers; and this criminal intercourse is carried on with so much security because both officer and trader are in the same political interest and under the same powerful protection—one, often a leading man in the borough, and the other a tool of those who represent it. Consequently many traders have withdrawn from London and put in for a share of the benefits and advantages of the outports."

The following, on the same subject, of later date (February 1749), from Mr. Collier at Bath to his agent in London, is not without significance : " You cant imagine how the company were, by the invention and propagation of villanous untruths, prepossessed against Sussex and Kent, as if the smugglers were tacitly encouraged and even protected, and in particular the name of the Duke of . . . . and his brother, &c., were treated with great licentiousness, and indeed all persons concerned in the Government."

(The following note is appended to this extract : " The above evidently refers to the Duke of Newcastle and his brother, the two principal members of the Government. The Duke was directly charged with conduct of this kind at the election of 1734. Horace Walpole, describing a Sussex tour, mentions a very high hill as that ' to the brow of which the Duke of Newcastle leads the smugglers, saying to them, " all

THE MURDERS BY SMUGGLERS 83

this will I give you if you will fall down and worship me." ' ")

September 10th, 1748, came news of the finding of the bodies of Galley and Chater, barbarously murdered by the Chichester smugglers last March : And in November of the capture of James Kemp and James Tough, two outlawed smugglers who had broken out of Newgate and had been concerned in the murder of the two men above-mentioned : Kemp having informed against the other. Also, in December comes news that one Stevens, a smuggler, who was taken when trying to escape to France, was carried before the Duke of Richmond, when he threw himself upon his knees, greatly terrified, and made full confession of the murder of Galley, recounting the horrible cruelties he inflicted on him. " This wretch, who is no more than 22, is now in Horsham Gaol."

On 19th December Elizabeth Payne and her two sons were committed to Winchester Gaol, as accomplices in the above murders. And on the 24th Mr. Collier's son-in-law writes him from Sussex : " I hear there will be special Assizes held in this county the middle of next month for trying the persons concerned in the murder of the two men in the West (Galley and Chater) and for trying other smugglers now in gaol, and that the Jury is to consist of the principal gentry of the County."

January 8th, 1749 Jackson and Carter, two of the outlawed smugglers concerned in the murder of the two men near Chichester, and confined in Newgate, " were brought into the press-yard, stripped and washed with vinegar, and afterwards dressed in two new suits of cloaths lent them by the Government : " next day they were ordered to Chichester Gaol.

January 16–17–18, 1749. Were arraigned, tried, and convicted of the murders of Galley and Chater, the seven smugglers previously apprehended, and executed at Chichester the following day. Young Mills was stated to have smiled several times at the hangman, who was a discharged marine, and whose ropes being too short for some of the smugglers, was puzzled to fit them. Old Mills, being forced to stand on tip-toe to reach the halter, desired that he might not be hanged by inches. It was very remarkable that the two Mills were so rejoiced on being told that they were not to be hanged in chains, that death seemed to excite no dread in them. Jackson, on the other hand, was struck with such terror on being measured for his irons that he expired soon after.

The two Mills, above mentioned, were the father and brother of John Mills, whose career and end has already been alluded to. They were natives of Trotton, where, until they took up with the smuggling, they carried on business as colt-breakers. The father, at one time, was well-to-do, and respected in the county, but after taking to smuggling, he lost his business and became poor; he was in receipt of parish relief, and though he had given up going down to the coast with the armed gangs, he still made a little by allowing goods to be stored in his house at Trotton. The son, who had been persuaded to take to smuggling by the old man, was a hardened and most desperate criminal. On being told, on the evening of his conviction, that they were all to be brought down to Court again, next morning, young Mills replied: "What the devil do they mean by that? could not they do the whole business this night, without obliging us to come again and wear

TRIAL OF SMUGGLERS 85

out our shoes?" At the place of execution he spent the time watching the preparations and gazing at the spectators, quite unconcernedly. The bodies of father and son, in default of friends to remove them, were thrown into a hole near the gallows, along with that of Jackson, and a stone was subsequently placed over the spot, bearing an inscription. The execution took place at the Broyle, about a mile out of Chichester.

The Solicitor to the Customs having written to Mr. Collier, under date February 21st, 1749 : " We have lived for these three months past under continued expectation of apprehending some more of the murderers, but I have not such an account as yet " ; Mr. Collier replies : " I well know the fatigue you had undergone in the prosecution and bringing to Justice the villains at Chichester whose cruelty . . . was beyond example, and more particularly so deliberate and premeditated in murder. . . . The Chichester Special Commission of Oyer and Terminer and the trials thereon shocked everybody, and was the subject of discourse for some time in the public Rooms, Coffee-houses and Parade " (at Bath where he was staying, for the benefit of his health).

Probably few trials of the eighteenth century caused such a sensation throughout the kingdom as the trial of the Hawkhurst gang of smugglers, at Chichester, in January 1749. An eye-witness thus wrote of it at the time : " Of all the monstrous wickedness with which this age abounds, nothing, I will be bound to say, can parallel the scenes of villainy that were laid bare. When the facts were proved by undeniable evidence in the face of the Court," he continues, " what horror and detestation appeared in the countenance of everyone present !

Everyone shuddered when they heard the aggravating circumstances of the murders related, and how barbarously the villains handled their wretched victims. The Judges themselves declared on the bench, that in all their reading, they never met with such a continued scene of barbarity, so deliberately carried on, and so cruelly executed."

Was it surprising, under these circumstances, that customs officers, magistrates, and everyone concerned in the maintenance of law and order were afraid to act? But though the worst of the ruffians had been sent to their account, the spirit of lawlessness was too deeply rooted and widespread to be much affected by their execution. Things soon resumed their normal course, and within a month we find a Mr. Worge writing to Mr. Collier, from Battle, March 17th: " Smuggling goes on as much as ever, and I am very much afraid they will soon get to carrying arms, for I hear they begin to grow insolent. The Halter has indeed pretty well cleared us of the outlawed chapps that committed so many Robberys and outrages in the County."

March 13th comes news of the arrest of one of the murderers of Mr. Carswell; thus Mr. Collier's clerk writes him: "Last Saturday Wm. Skinner, one of the Goudhurst Militia, and another, informed me that Polhill and others, assisted by Dragoons, had, on the 6th of this month, apprehended about three miles from Maidstone John Boscell, a notorious smuggler who stands indicted for the murder of my wife's Father, Carsewell."

During the month of March one smuggler was condemned to death for horse-stealing, and three others for burglary and highway robbery; also seven outlawed smugglers, for being concerned in

TRIAL OF SMUGGLERS

various murders and outrages, were sentenced to be hanged.

A contemporary journal, commenting on the late trials, observed: " The great mischief done of late by the smugglers is in part to be accounted for by the decline of their business. The profits of smuggling a few years ago were so considerable, occasioned by the high duties, that the very hirelings had such extravagant gains, as were sufficient to corrupt the most industrious labourer from his honest employment: each man being allowed half a guinea each journey and a dollop of tea weighing 13lb., besides having a horse found them and their expenses borne. As they generally ran two cargoes a week, their gains bore no proportion to the price of common labour; but of late that trade has taken a different turn, and the dealers in it are reduced to the greatest extremities."

During April three of the smugglers concerned in the breaking open of Poole custom-house received sentence. Concerning whom, Mr. Collier, still at Bath for his health, received the following letter from his clerk: " Some time ago, a person these villains suspected to have been an informer was, at or near Tarring in this county, barbarously beat and abused by them. . . . George Chapman, one of the most notorious concerned in the murder of Mr. Carswell, is apprehended and committed to Maidstone Gaol. He was taken by Drury of Robertsbridge and the Goudhurst Militia. I am informed that John Boscall has been admitted as evidence, he having made a full discovery of the whole affair and has impeached the whole gang." And on May 23rd the same correspondent writes: " The inhabitants of Hastings were much incensed at one Harrison for informing against several persons in Hastings and elsewhere for being concerned with him in smuggling practices; and that one Evers had been arrested on Harrison's information. I am afraid Harrison has acted indiscreetly, particularly in getting drunk before he left this town, Saturday night, insomuch that he was not able to ride with Polhill and the Dragoons any further than a little alehouse about a quarter of a mile from Fairlight church, where he got off his horse and went to sleep in a chair, and the worthy Mr. Grayling and several others having intelligence that Harrison was asleep at that house, went forthwith thither full of Revenge and Malice, but fortunately for Harrison, he was awakened out of sleep, and gone by Rye, about 2 or 3 minutes before Grayling came to Bridgers. I am really surprised," adds the writer, with well-feigned ingenuousness, " to see what a spirit of smuggling is grafted in this town; for the apprehension of Evers has put the inhabitants in the greatest flame imaginable; for I am really of opinion that nine parts in ten thereof would as freely murder Harrison as they would eat or drink when hungry or dry." And he goes on to acquaint Mr. Collier that Evers, on being arrested, sent to his brother-in-law to say he was willing to become evidence along with Harrison, and begging to be recommended for favour on those terms.

During July, James Toby, an old smuggler, was convicted for carrying wool to France. It was further proved that he held a correspondence with the French during the late Rebellion, and not only furnished them with wool, but swivel-guns for their privateers. Also, two other smugglers were sentenced to be executed.

During August six smugglers were condemned: viz. one for the murder of Galley; two for the murder of Thomas Carswell, riding-officer (in 1740), and three for the murder of a Dragoon in 1743.

October 31st. At Hastings, while searching a house for goods, was discovered in bed, feigning sick, John French, an outlawed smuggler, one of the first persons advertised in the *Gazette* for running goods with fire-arms at Sea-houses, near Eastbourne, for which Ashcraft had been executed.

To judge from what follows, it would seem as if the imputations against certain riding-officers, of connivance with smuggling, were not altogether baseless. The Solicitor of the Customs writes Mr. Collier (March 20th, 1749): "Stanford (alias Tripp), finding his tryall fixd, as far as I can understand begins to squeek, and it has been hinted to me that his first discovery will be of their keeping a good understanding, for a valuable consideration, with many of the Rideing officers along the coast, higher up in the country and just in the neighbourhood of the Town. This, if true, will make sad work, though at the same time such a collusion is truly infamous and the actors in it cannot but fall unpitied."

So deeply-rooted was the evil that when, many years later, Pitt set himself to tackle the smugglers, he was under the necessity, before reform could be introduced, of proclaiming a general amnesty. For the Revenue officers, everywhere along the coast, by their connivance, had placed themselves so completely in the power of the smugglers, that the Government had to relieve its servants from all fear of the consequences of their own actions.

During November comes word from Boulogne that many outlawed and other smugglers flock thither and are forming themselves into a company to promote smuggling.

Next year (November 15th, 1750) a Colonel Fuller, residing in Sussex, writes to Mr. Collier with reference to some smugglers breaking open the Custom House at Rye : " You know very well, as Tea is now grown one meal in 3 of almost all the people in England, especially in the South, and as the India Company have the monopoly and sell it for a 3d. dearer than the rest of Europe, that this pernitious practice must continue, and will soon be beyond the power of the Ministry to check, or the more prevayling power of Hemp. I expect, the first set that are informed against, that murders, robberies, &c. will be as brisk as ever." Mr. Collier, in his reply, says that he had not heard of any instance of gangs riding about armed, and committing such depredations as they had done about four or five years since; though there was a gang in and about the parish of Hooe who seemed to have no other means of livelihood.

A letter of March 20th, 1753, throws an interesting light on contemporary manners. Mr. Collier writes, with reference to an approaching trial of smugglers : " As in cases of this nature the smugglers and their well-wishers frequently throng the Court to be ready to serve on the Jury, it's hoped that the Jurys to try the prisoners may be persons of reputation and credit, not tainted with smuggling practices."

The following, written by Mr. Collier to his London agent, shortly before the outbreak of the " Seven Years' War " with France, is not devoid of interest in view of the important part played by the smugglers in keeping up an illicit correspondence : " Our intelligence from the French coast is at present over, for

'RUXLEY'S CREW' 91

all our smuggling Rascalls with their vessels are seized at Boulogne, Calais, and Dunkirk, &c." (February 26th, 1756).

Mr. Collier having now reached his seventy-first year, and being in failing health, resigned his post of Surveyor-General of the Customs for the Counties of Kent and Sussex, and the interesting correspondence terminated. He was succeeded in the post by his son-in-law, Mr. Milward. Yet did the spirit of lawlessness prevail in this "nest of vermin"; and the world was startled two years later by a fresh chapter of horrors, brought to light during the trial of a gang of pirates and sea ruffians known as "Ruxley's crew"; or, alternatively, as "Ruxley's gang," belonging chiefly to Hastings.

CHAPTER IV

THE "MURDERS BY SMUGGLERS" IN HAMPSHIRE

THE most outstanding chapter in the whole history of smuggling is that of the cold-blooded "Murders by Smugglers" which stained the annals of the southern counties in the mid-eighteenth century with peculiarly revolting deeds that have in them nothing of romance; nothing but a long-drawn story of villainy and fiendish cruelty. It is a story that long made dwellers in solitary situations shiver with apprehension, especially if they owned relatives connected in any way with the hated customs officers.

This grim chapter of horrors, upon which the historian can dwell only with loathing, and with pity for himself in being brought to the telling of it, is the subject of scattered allusions in the Collier correspondence already quoted. The affair was the direct outcome of the lawless and almost unchecked doings of the Hawkhurst gang, whose daring grew continually with their long-continued success in terrorising the countryside.

The beginnings of this affair are found in an expedition entered upon by a number of the gang in September 1747, in Guernsey, where they purchased a considerable quantity of tea, for smuggling into this country. Unfortunately for their enterprise, they fell in with a revenue cutter, commanded by one Captain Johnson, who pursued and captured

A Representation of ye Smuglers breaking open ye Kings Custom House at Poole.

GALLEY AND CHATER

their vessel, took it into the port of Poole, and lodged the tea in the custom-house there.

The smugglers were equally incensed and dismayed at this disaster, the loss being a very heavy one; and they resolved, rather than submit to it, to go in an armed force and recover the goods. Accordingly a mounted body of them, to the number of sixty, well provided with firearms and other weapons, assembled in Charlton Forest, and thence proceeded on their desperate errand. Thirty of them, it was agreed, should go to the attack, while the other thirty should take up positions as scouts along the various roads, to watch for riding-officers, or for any military force, and so alarm, or actively assist, if needs were, the attacking party.

It was in the midnight between October 6th and 7th that this advance party reached Poole, broke open the custom-house on the quay, and removed all the captured tea—thirty-seven hundredweight, valued at £500—except one bag of about five pounds weight. They returned in the morning, in leisurely fashion, through Fordingbridge; the affair apparently so public that hundreds of people were assembled in the streets of that little town to see these daring fellows pass.

Among these spectators was one Daniel Chater, a shoemaker, who recognised among this cavalcade of smugglers a certain John Diamond, with whom he had formerly worked in the harvest field. Diamond shook hands with him as he passed, and threw him a bag of tea.

It was not long before a proclamation was issued offering rewards for the identification or apprehension of any persons concerned in this impudent raid, and Diamond was in the meanwhile arrested on suspicion at Chichester. Chater, who seems to have been a foolish, gossiping fellow, saying he knew Diamond and saw him go by with the gang, became an object of considerable interest to his neighbours at Fordingbridge, who, having seen that present of a bag of tea—a very considerable present as the price of tea then ran—no doubt thought he knew more of the affair than he cared to tell. At any rate, these things came to the knowledge of the Collector of Customs at Southampton, and the upshot of several interviews and some correspondence with him was that Chater agreed to go in company with one William Galley, an officer of excise, to Major Battin, a Justice of the Peace and a Commissioner of Customs at Chichester, to be examined as to his readiness and ability to identify Diamond, whose punishment, on conviction, would be, under the savage laws of that time, death.

Chater, in short, had offered himself as that detestable thing, a hired informer : a creature all right-minded men abhor, and whom the smugglers of that age visited, whenever found, with persecution and often with the same extremity to which the law doomed themselves.

The ill-fated pair set out on Sunday, February 14th, on horseback, and, calling on their way at Havant, were directed by a friend of Chater's at that place to go by way of Stanstead, near Rowlands Castle. They soon, however, missed their way, and calling at Leigh, at the " New Inn," to refresh and to inquire the road, met there three men, George and Thomas Austin, and their brother-in-law, one Mr. Jenkes, who accompanied them to Rowlands Castle, where they all drew rein at the " White Hart " public-house, kept by a Mrs. Elizabeth

AT THE 'WHITE HART'   95

Payne, a widow, who had two sons in the village, blacksmiths, and both reputed smugglers.

Some rum was called for, and was being drank, when Mrs. Payne, taking George Austin aside, told him she was afraid these two strangers were after no good; they had come, she suspected, with intent to do some injury to the smugglers. Such was the state of the rural districts in those times that the appearance of two strangers was of itself a cause for distrust; but when, in addition, there was the damning fact that one of them wore the uniform of a riding-officer of excise, suspicion became almost a certainty.

But to her remarks George Austin replied she need not be alarmed, the strangers were only carrying a letter to Major Battin, on some ordinary official business.

This explanation, however, served only to increase her suspicions, for what more likely than that this business with a man who was, among other things, a highly placed customs official, was connected in some way with these recent notorious happenings?

To make sure, Mrs. Payne sent privately one of her sons, who was then in the house, for William Jackson and William Carter, two men deeply involved with smuggling, who lived near at hand. In the meanwhile Chater and Galley wanted to be gone upon their journey, and asked for their horses. Mrs. Payne, to keep them until Jackson and Carter should arrive, told them the man who had the key of the stables was gone for a while, but would return presently.

As the unsuspecting men waited, gossiping and drinking, the two smugglers entered. Mrs. Payne drew them aside and whispered her suspicions;

at the same time advising Mr. George Austin to go away, as she respected him, and was unwilling that any harm should come to him.

It is thus sufficiently clear that, even at this early stage, some very serious mischief was contemplated. Mr. George Austin, being a prudent, if certainly not also an honest, man, did as he was advised. Thomas Austin, his brother, who does not appear to have in the same degree commanded the landlady's respect, was not warned, and remained, together with his brother-in-law. To have won the reader's respect also, she should, at the very least of it, have warned them as well. But as this was obviously not a school of morals, we will not labour the point, and will bid Mr. George Austin, with much relief, "good-bye."

Mrs. Payne's other son then entered, bringing with him four more smugglers: William Steel, Samuel Downer, *alias* Samuel Howard, *alias* "Little Sam," Edmund Richards, and Henry Sheerman, *alias* "Little Harry."

After a while Jackson took Chater aside into the yard, and asked him after Diamond; whereupon the simple-minded man let fall the object of his and his companion's journey.

While they were talking, Galley suspecting Chater would be in some way indiscreet, came out and asked him to rejoin them; whereupon Jackson, with a horrible oath, struck him a violent blow in the face, knocking him down.

Galley then rushed into the house, Jackson following him. "I am a King's officer," exclaimed the unfortunate Galley, "and cannot put up with such treatment."

"You a King's officer!" replied Jackson, "I'll

Chater, Chained in y̅e̅ Turff House at Old Mills.
Cobby, kicking him, & Tapner, cutting him Cross y̅e̅
Eyes & Nose, while he is saying the Lords Prayer
Several of y̅e̅ other Smugglers standing by.

COUNCIL OF MURDERERS

make a King's Officer of you; and for a quartern of gin I'll serve you so again!"

The others interposed, one of the Paynes exclaiming, "Don't be such a fool; do you know what you are doing?"

Galley and Chater grew very uneasy, and again wanted to be going; but the company present, including Jackson, pressed them to stay, Jackson declaring he was sorry for what had passed. The entire party then sat down to more drink, until Galley and Chater were overcome by drunkenness and were sent to sleep in an adjoining room. Thomas Austin and Mr. Jenkes were by this time also hopelessly drunk; but as they had no concern with the smugglers, nor the smugglers with them, they drop out of this narrative.

When Galley and Chater lay in their drunken sleep the compromising letters in their pockets were found and read, and the men present formed themselves into a kind of committee to decide what should be done with their enemies, as they thought them. John Race and Richard Kelly then came in, and Jackson and Carter told them they had got the old rogue, the shoemaker of Fordingbridge, who was going to give an information against John Diamond the shepherd, then in custody at Chichester.

They then consulted what was best to be done to their two prisoners, when William Steel proposed to take them both to a well, a little way from the house, and to murder them and throw them in. Less ferocious proposals were made—to send them over to France; but when it became obvious that they would return and give the evidence after all, the thoughts of the seven men present reverted to murder. At this juncture the wives of Jackson and

Carter, who had entered the house, cried, " Hang the dogs, for they came here to hang us ! "

Another proposition that was made—to imprison the two in some safe place until they knew what would be Diamond's fate, and for each of the smugglers to subscribe threepence a week for their keep—was immediately scouted; and instantly the brutal fury of these ruffians was aroused by Jackson, who, going into the room where the unfortunate men were lying, spurred them on their foreheads with the heavy spurs of his riding-boots, and, having thus effectually wakened them, whipped them into the kitchen of the inn until they were streaming with blood. Then, taking them outside, the gang lifted them on to a horse, one behind the other, and, tying their hands and legs together, lashed them with heavy whips along the road, crying, " Whip them, cut them, slash them, damn them ! " one of their number, Edmund Richards, with cocked pistol in hand, swearing he would shoot any person through the head who should mention anything of what he saw or heard.

From Rowlands Castle, past Wood Ashes, Goodthorpe Deane, and to Lady Holt Park, this scourging was continued through the night, until the wretched men were three-parts dead. At two o'clock in the morning this gruesome procession reached the Portsmouth Road at Rake, where the foremost members of the party halted at what was then the " Red Lion " inn, long since that time retired into private life, and now a humble cottage. It was kept in those days by one Scardefield, who was no stranger to their kind, nor unused to the purchase and storing of smuggled spirits. Here they knocked and rattled at the door until Scardefield was obliged

AT THE 'RED LION'

to get out of bed and open to them. Galley, still alive, was thrust into an outhouse, while the band, having roused the landlord and procured drink, caroused in the parlour of the inn. Chater they carried in with them; and when Scardefield stood horrified at seeing so ghastly a figure of a man, all bruised and broken, and spattered with blood, they told him a specious tale of an engagement they had had with the King's officers : that here was a comrade, wounded, and another, dead or dying, in his brewhouse.

Chater they presently carried to an outhouse of the cottage of a man named Mills, not far off, and then returned for more drink and discussion of what was to be done with Galley, whom they decided to bury in Harting Combe. So, while it was yet dark, they carried him down from the ridge on which Rake stands, into the valley, and, digging a grave in a fox-earth by the light of a lantern, shovelled the dirt over him, without inquiring too closely whether their victim were alive or dead. That he was not dead at that time became evident when his body was discovered eight months later, hands raised to his face, as though to prevent the earth from suffocating him.

The whole of the next day this evil company sat drinking in the "Red Lion." Richard Mills, son of the man in whose turf-shed Chater lay chained by the leg, passing by, they hailed him and told him of what they had done; whereupon he said he would, if he had had the doing of it, have flung the man down Harting Combe headlong and broken his neck.

On this Monday night they all returned home, lest their continued absence might be remarked by the neighbours; agreeing to meet again at Rake on the Wednesday evening, to consider how they might best put an end to Chater.

When Wednesday night had come this council of murderers, reinforced by others, and numbering in all fourteen, assembled accordingly. Dropping into the " Red Lion " one by one, it was late at night before they had all gathered.

They decided, after some argument, to dispatch him forthwith, and, going down to the turf-shed where he had lain all this while, suffering agonies from the cruel usage to which he had been subjected, they unchained him. Richard Mills at first had proposed to finish him there. " Let us," he said, " load a gun with two or three bullets, lay it upon a stand with the muzzle of the piece levelled at his head, and, after having tied a long string to the trigger we will all go off to the butt-end, and, each of us taking hold of the string, pull it all together; thus we shall be all equally guilty of his death, and it will be impossible for any one of us to charge the rest with his murder, without accusing himself of the same crime; and none can pretend to lessen or to mitigate his guilt by saying he was only an accessory, since all will be principals."

Thus Richard Mills, according to the story of these things told in horrid detail (together with a full report of the subsequent trial) by the author of the contemporary " Genuine History." The phraseology of the man's coldly logical proposals is, of course, that of the author himself; since it is not possible that a Sussex rustic of over a hundred and sixty years ago would have spoken in literary English.

Mills's proposition was not accepted. It seemed to the others too merciful and expeditious a method

THE "RED LION," RAKE

IN LADY HOLT PARK

of putting an end to Chater's misery. They had grown as epicurean in torture as the mediæval hell-hounds who racked and pinched and burnt for Church and State. They were resolved he should suffer as much and as long as they could eke out his life, as a warning to all other informers.

The proposal that found most favour was that they should take him to Harris's Well, in Lady Holt Park, and throw him in.

Tapner, one of the recruits to the gang, thereupon inaugurated the new series of torments by pulling out a large clasp-knife, and, with a fearful oath, exclaiming, " Down on your knees and go to prayers, for with this knife I will be your butcher."

Chater, expecting every moment to be his last, knelt down as he was ordered, and, while he was thus praying, Cobby kicked him from behind, while Tapner in front slashed his face.

The elder Mills, owner of the turf-shed, at this grew alarmed for his own safety. " Take him away," he said, " and do not murder him here. Do it somewhere else."

They then mounted him on a horse and set out for Lady Holt Park; Tapner, more cruel, if possible, than the rest, slashing him with his knife, and whipping him with his whip, all the way.

It was dead of night by the time they had come to the Park, where there was a deep dry well. A wooden fence stretched across the track leading to it, and over this, although it was in places broken and could easily have been crawled through, they made their victim climb. Tapner then pulled a rope out of his pocket and tied it round Chater's neck, and so pushed him over the opening of the well, where he hung, slowly strangling.

But by this time they were anxious to get home, and could afford no more time for these luxuries of cruelty, so they dropped him to the bottom of the well, imagining he would be quite killed by the fall. Unfortunately for Chater, he was remarkably tenacious of life, and was heard groaning there, where he had fallen.

They dared not leave him thus, lest anyone passing should hear his cries, and went and roused a gardener, one William Combleach, who lived a little way off, and borrowed a ladder, telling him one of their companions had fallen into Harris's Well. With this ladder they intended to descend the well and finally dispatch Chater; but, seeing they could not manage to lower the ladder, they were reduced to finding some huge stones and two great gateposts, which they then flung down, and so ended the unhappy man's martyrdom.

The problem that next faced the murderers was, how to dispose of the two horses their victims had been riding. It was first proposed to put them aboard the next smuggling vessel returning to France, but that idea was abandoned, on account of the risk of discovery. It was finally decided to slaughter them and remove their skins, and this was accordingly done to the grey that Galley had ridden, and his hide cut up into small pieces and buried; but, when they came to look for the bay that Chater had used, they could not find him.

CHAPTER V

THE " MURDERS BY SMUGGLERS " *continued*—TRIAL AND EXECUTION OF THE MURDERERS—FURTHER CRIMES BY THE HAWKHURST GANG

EVEN in those times two men, and especially men who had set out upon official business, could not disappear so utterly as Chater and Galley had done without comment being aroused, and presently the whole country was ringing with the news of this mysterious disappearance. The condition of the country can at once be guessed when it is stated that no one doubted the hands of the smugglers in this business. The only question was, In what manner had they spirited these two men away? Some thought they had been carried over to France, while others thought, shrewdly enough, they had been murdered.

But no tidings nor any trace of either Galley or Chater came to satisfy public curiosity, or to allay official apprehensions, until some seven months later, when an anonymous letter sent to " a person of distinction," and probably inspired by the hope of ultimately earning the large reward offered by the Government for information, hinted that " the body of one of the unfortunate men mentioned in his Majesty's proclamation was buried in the sands in a certain place near Rake." And, sure enough, when search was made, the body of Galley was found "standing almost upright, with his hands covering his eyes."

Another letter followed upon this discovery, implicating William Steel in these doings, and he was immediately arrested. To save himself, the prisoner turned King's evidence, and revealed the whole dreadful story. John Race, among the others concerned, voluntarily surrendered, and was also admitted as evidence.

One after another, seven of the murderers were arrested in different parts of the counties of Hants and Surrey, and were committed to the gaols of Horsham and Newgate, afterwards being sent to Chichester, where a special Assize was held for the purpose of overawing the smugglers of the district, and of impressing them with the majesty and the power of the law, which, it was desired to show them, would eventually overtake all evil-doers.

We need not enter into the details of that trial, held on January 18th, 1749, and reported with painful elaboration by the author of the "Genuine History," together with the sermon preached in Chichester Cathedral by Dean Ashburnham, who held forth in the obvious and conventional way of comfortably beneficed clergy, then and now.

Let it be sufficient to say that all were found guilty, and all sentenced to be hanged on the following day.

Six of them were duly executed, William Jackson, the seventh, dying in gaol. He had been for a considerable time in ill health. He was a Roman Catholic and the greatest villain of the gang, and, like all such, steeped in superstition. Carefully sewed up in a linen purse in his waistcoat pocket was

found an amulet in French, which, translated, ran as follows :
> Ye three Holy Kings,
> Gaspar, Melchior, Balthasar,
> Pray for us now, and in the hour of death.
> These papers have touched the three heads of the Holy Kings at Cologne.
> They are to preserve travellers from accidents on the road, headaches, falling sickness, fevers, witchcraft, all kinds of mischief, and sudden death.

His body was thrown into a pit on the Broyle, at Chichester, together with those of Richard Mills, the elder, and younger. The body of William Carter was hanged in chains upon the Portsmouth road, near Rake; that of Benjamin Tapner on Rook's Hill, near Chichester, and those of John Cobby and John Hammond upon the sea-coast near Selsea Bill, so that they might be seen for great distances by any contrabandists engaged in running goods.

Another accomplice, Henry Shurman, or Sheerman, *alias* " Little Harry," was indicted and tried at East Grinstead, and, being sentenced to death, was conveyed to Horsham Gaol by a strong guard of soldiers and hanged at Rake, and afterwards gibbeted.

In January 1749, was committed the brutal murder at the " Dog and Partridge " inn, on Slindon Common, near Arundel, already referred to in the official correspondence; where Richard Hawkins was whipped and kicked to death on suspicion of being concerned in stealing two bags of tea belonging to one Jerry Curtis. Hawkins was enticed away from his work at Walberton, on some specious pretext, by Curtis and John Mills, known as " Smoker," and went on horseback behind Mills to the " Dog and Partridge," where they joined a man named Robb :

all these men being well-known smugglers in that district. Having safely got Hawkins thus far, they informed him that he was their prisoner, and proceeded to put him under examination in the parlour of the inn. There were also present Thomas Winter (afterwards a witness for the prosecution) and James Reynolds, the innkeeper.

Hawkins denied having stolen the tea, and said he knew nothing of the matter, whereupon Curtis replied, " Damn you; you do know, and if you do not confess I will whip you till you do; for, damn you, I have whipped many a rogue and washed my hands in his blood."

Reynolds said, " Dick, you had better confess; it will be better for you." But his answer still was, " I know nothing of it."

Reynolds then went out, and Mills and Robb thereupon beat and kicked Hawkins so ferociously that he cried out that the Cockrels, his father-in-law and brother-in-law, who kept an inn at Yapton, were concerned in it. Curtis and Mills then took their horses and said they would go and fetch them. Going to the younger Cockrel, Mills entered the house first and called for some ale. Then Curtis came in and demanded his two bags of tea, which he said Hawkins had accused him of having. Cockrel denied having them, and then Curtis beat him with an oak stick until he was tired. Curtis and Mills then forcibly took him to where his father was, at Walberton, and thence, with his father, behind them on their horses, towards Slindon.

Meanwhile, at the " Dog and Partridge," Robb and Winter placed the terribly injured man, Hawkins, in a chair by the fire, where he died.

Robb and Winter then took their own horses and

John Mills alias Smoaker, & Rich.ᵈ Rowland alias Robb, Whipping Rich.ᵈ Hawkins, to Death, at yͤ Dog & Partridge on Slendon Common; & Jeremiah Curtis, & Tho.ˢ Winter alias Coachman, Standing by Aiding & abetting yͤ Murder of the said Rich.ᵈ Hawkins.

rode out towards Yapton, meeting Curtis and Mills on the way, each with a man behind him. The men, who were the Cockrels, were told to get off, which they did, and the four others held a whispered conversation, when Winter told them that Hawkins was dead, and desired them to do no more mischief.

"By God!" exclaimed Curtis, "we will go through it now." Winter again urged them to be content with what had already been done; and Curtis then bade the two Cockrels return home.

Then they all four rode back to the "Dog and Partridge," where Reynolds was in despair, saying to Curtis, "You have ruined me."

Curtis replied that he would make him amends; and they all then consulted how to dispose of the body. The first proposition was to bury it in a park close at hand, and to give out that the smugglers had deported Hawkins to France. But Reynolds objected. The spot, he said, was too near, and would soon be found. In the end, they laid the body on a horse and carried it to Parham Park, twelve miles away, where they tied large stones to it, and sunk it in a pond.

This crime was in due course discovered, and a proclamation issued, offering a pardon to anyone, not himself concerned in the murder, nor in the breaking open of the custom-house at Poole, who should give information that would lead to the capture and conviction of the offenders.

John Mills was a son of Richard Mills, and a brother of Richard Mills the younger, executed at Chichester for the murder of Chater and Galley, as already detailed, and he also had taken part in that business. Brought to trial at East Grinstead, he said he had indeed been a very wicked liver, but he bitterly complained of such of the witnesses against him as had been smugglers and had turned King's evidence. They had, he declared, acted contrary from the solemn oaths and engagements they had made and sworn to among themselves, and he therefore wished they might all come to the same end, and be hanged like him and damned afterwards.

He was found guilty and duly sentenced to death, and was hanged and afterwards hung in chains on a gibbet erected for the purpose on Slindon Common, near the " Dog and Partridge."

Curtis, an active partner in the same murder, fled the country, and was said to have enlisted in the Irish Brigade of the French Army. Robb was not taken, and Reynolds was acquitted of the murder. He and his wife were tried at the next Assizes, as accessories after the fact.

The " Dog and Partridge " has long ceased to be an inn, but the house survives, a good deal altered, as a cottage. In the garden may be seen a very capacious cellar, excavated out of the soil and sandstone, and very much larger than a small country inn could have ever required for ordinary business purposes. It is known as the " Smugglers' Cellar."

At the same sessions at which these blood-stained scoundrels were convicted a further body of five men, Lawrence and Thomas Kemp, John Brown, Robert Fuller, and Richard Savage, were all tried on charges of highway robbery, of house-breaking, and of stealing goods from a wagon. They were all members of the notorious Hawkhurst gang, and had been smugglers for many years. All were found guilty and sentenced to death, except Savage, who was awarded transportation for life. The rest were executed at Horsham on April 1st, 1749. One of

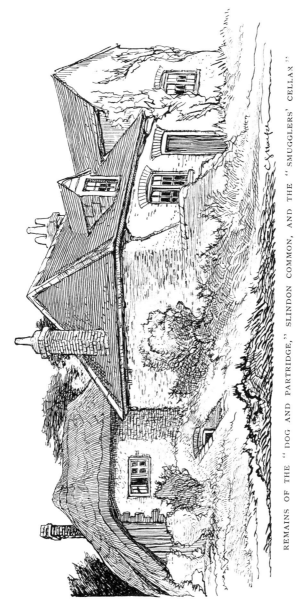

REMAINS OF THE "DOG AND PARTRIDGE," SLINDON COMMON, AND THE "SMUGGLERS' CELLAR"

them had at least once already come near to being capitally convicted, but had been rescued from Newgate by a party of fellow-smugglers before justice could complete her processes.

These rescuers were in their turn arrested on other charges, and brought to trial at Rochester Assizes, with other malefactors, in March 1750. They were four notorious smugglers, Stephen Diprose, James Bartlett, Thomas Potter, and William Priggs, who were all executed on Penenden Heath, on March 30th.

Bartlett, pressed to declare, after sentence, if he had been concerned in any murders, particularly in that of Mr. Castle, an excise officer who had been shot on Selhurst Common by a gang of smugglers, would not give a positive answer, and it was therefore supposed he was concerned in it.

Potter described some of the doings of the gang, and told how, fully armed, they would roam the country districts at night, disguised, with blackened faces, and appear at lonely houses, where they would seize and bind the people they found, and then proceed to plunder at their leisure.

In the short interval that in those days was allowed between sentence and execution Potter was very communicative, and disclosed a long career of crime; but he declared that murder had never been committed by him. He had, it was true, proposed to murder the turnkey at Newgate at the time when he and his companions rescued their friends languishing in that doleful hold; but it had not, after all, been found necessary.

This, it will be conceded, was sufficiently frank and open. The official account of that rescue has already been set forth in the preceding pages.

All these men were, in fact, originally smugglers,

and had, from being marked down as criminals for that offence, and from being "wanted" by the law, found themselves obliged to keep in hiding from their homes. In default of being able to take part in other runs of smuggled goods, and finding themselves unable to get employment, they were driven to other, and more serious, crimes.

On April 4th of the same year four other members of the terrible Hawkhurst gang—Kingsmill, Fairall, Perrin, and Glover by name—were together brought to trial at the Old Bailey, charged with being concerned in the Poole affair, the breaking open of the custom-house, and the stealing of goods therefrom. They had been betrayed to the Government by the same two ex-smugglers who had turned King's evidence at the Chichester trial, and their evidence again secured a conviction. Glover, recommended by the jury to the royal mercy, was eventually pardoned; but the remaining three were hanged. Fairall behaved most insolently at the trial and even threatened one of the witnesses. Glover displayed penitence; and Kingsmill and Perrin insisted that they had not been guilty of any robbery, because the goods they had taken were their own.

Kingsmill had been leader in the ferocious attack on Goudhurst in April 1747, and was an extremely dangerous ruffian, ready for any extremity.

Fairall was proved to be a particularly desperate fellow. Two years earlier he had been apprehended, as a smuggler, in Sussex, and, being brought before Mr. Butler, a magistrate, at Lewes, was remitted by him for trial in London.

Brought under escort over-night to the New Prison in the Borough, Fairall found means to make a dash from the custody of his guards, and, leaping upon a

PROPOSED OUTRAGES

horse that was standing in Blackman Street, rode away and escaped, within sight of numerous people.

Returning to the gang, who were reasonably surprised at his safe return from the jaws of death, he was filled with an unreasoning hatred of Mr. Butler, the justice who, in the ordinary course of his duty, had committed him. He proposed a complete and terrible revenge : firstly, by destroying all the deer in his park, and all his trees, which was readily agreed to by the gang; and then, since those measures were not extreme enough for them, the idea was discussed of setting fire to his house and burning him alive in it. Some of the conspirators, however, thought this too extreme a step, and they parted without coming to any decision. Fairall, Kingsmill, and others, however, determined not to be baulked, then each procured a brace of pistols, and waited for the magistrate, near his own park wall, to shoot him when he returned home that night from a journey to Horsham.

Fortunately for him, some accident kept him from returning, and the party of would-be assassins, tired of waiting, at last said to one another, " Damn him, he will not come home to-night ! Let us be gone about our business." They then dispersed, swearing they would watch for a month together, but they would have him; and that they would make an example of all who should dare to obstruct them.

Perrin's body was directed to be given to his friends, instead of being hanged in chains, and he was pitying the misfortunes of his two companions, who were not only, like himself, to be hanged, but whose bodies were afterwards to be gibbeted, when Fairall said, " *We* shall be hanging up in the sweet air when *you* are rotting in your grave."

Fairall kept a bold front to the very last. The night before the execution, he smoked continually with his friends, until ordered by the warder to go to his cell; when he exclaimed, "Why in such a hurry? Cannot you let me stay a little longer with my friends? I shall not be able to drink with them to-morrow night."

But perhaps there was more self-pity in those apparently careless words and in that indifferent demeanour than those thought who heard them.

Kingsmill was but twenty-eight years of age, and Fairall twenty-five, at the time of their execution, which took place at Tyburn on April 26th, 1749. Fairall's body was hanged in chains on Horsenden Green, and that of Kingsmill on Goudhurst Gore, appropriately near the frighted village whose inhabitants he had promised the vengeance of himself and his reckless band.

Scarcely any one of the maritime counties, says G. P. R. James, author of that romance, *The Smuggler*, was without its gang of smugglers; for if France was not opposite, Holland was not far off; and if brandy was not the object, nor silk, nor wine, yet tea and cinnamon, and hollands, and various East India goods, were duly estimated by the British public, especially when they could be obtained without the payment of custom-house dues.

As there are land-sharks and water-sharks, so there were land-smugglers and water-smugglers. The latter brought the objects of their commerce either from foreign countries or from foreign vessels, and landed them on the coast—and a bold, daring, reckless body of men they were; the former, in gangs, consisting frequently of many hundreds, generally well-mounted and armed, conveyed the commodities so landed into the interior and distributed them to others, who retailed them as occasion required. Nor were these gentry one whit less fearless, enterprising, and lawless than their brethren of the sea.

The ramifications of this vast and magnificent league extended themselves to almost every class of society. Each tradesman smuggled, or dealt in smuggled goods; each public-house was supported by smugglers, and gave them in return every facility possible; each country gentleman on the coast dabbled a little in the interesting traffic; almost every magistrate shared in the proceeds, or partook of the commodities. Scarcely a house but had its place of concealment, which would accommodate either kegs or bales, or human beings, as the case might be; and many streets in seaport towns had private passages from one house to another, so that the gentleman inquired for by the officers at No. 1 was often walking quietly out of No. 20, while they were searching for him in vain. The back of one street had always excellent means of communication with the front of another, and the gardens gave exit to the country with as little delay as possible.

Of all counties, however, the most favoured by nature and art for the very pleasant and exciting sport of smuggling was the county of Kent. Its geographical position, its local features, its variety of coast, all afforded it the greatest advantages, and the daring character of the natives on the shores of the Channel was sure to turn those advantages to the purposes in question. Sussex, indeed, was not without its share of facilities, nor did the Sussex men fail to improve them; but they were so much farther off from the opposite coast that the chief commerce—the regular trade—was not in any degree at Hastings, Rye, or Winchelsea to be compared with that carried on from the North Foreland to Romney Hoy. At one time the fine level of the Marsh, a dark night, and a fair wind, afforded a delightful opportunity for landing a cargo and carrying it rapidly into the interior; at another, Sandwich Flats and Pevensey Bay presented harbours of refuge and places of repose for kegs innumerable and bales of great value; at another, the cliffs round Folkestone and near the South Foreland saw spirits travelling up by paths which seemed inaccessible to mortal foot; and at another, the wild and broken ground at the back of Sandgate was traversed by long trains of horses, escorting or carrying every description of contraband articles.

The interior of the county was not less favourable to the traffic than the coast: large masses of wood, numerous gentlemen's parks, hills and dales tossed about in wild confusion; roads such as nothing but horses could travel, or men on foot, often constructed with felled trees or broad stones laid side by side; wide tracts of ground, partly copse and partly moor, called in that county "minnises," and a long extent of the Weald of Kent, through which no highway existed, and where such a thing as coach or carriage was never seen, offered the land-smugglers opportunities of carrying on their transactions with a degree of secrecy and safety no other county afforded. Their numbers, too, were so great, their boldness and violence so notorious, their powers of injuring or annoying so various, that even those who took no part in their operations were glad to connive at their proceedings, and at times to aid in concealing their persons or their goods. Not a park, not a wood, not a barn, that did not at some period afford them a refuge when pursued, or become a depository for their commodities, and many a man, on visiting his stables or his cart-shed early in the morning, found it tenanted by anything but horses or wagons. The churchyards were frequently crowded at night by other spirits than those of the dead, and not even the church was exempted from such visitations.

None of the people of the county took notice of or opposed these proceedings. The peasantry laughed at, or aided, and very often got a good day's work, or, at all events, a jug of genuine hollands, from the friendly smugglers; the clerk and the sexton willingly aided and abetted, and opened the door of vault, or vestry, or church for the reception of the passing goods; the clergyman shut his eyes if he saw tubs or jars in his way; and it is remarkable what good brandy-punch was generally to be found at the house of the village pastor. The magistrates of the county, when called upon to aid in pursuit of the smugglers, looked grave and swore in constables very slowly, dispatched servants on horseback to see what was going on, and ordered the steward or the butler to "send the sheep to the wood": an intimation not lost upon those for whom it was intended. The magistrates and officers of seaport towns were in general so deeply implicated in the trade themselves that smuggling had a fairer chance than the law in any case that came before them; and never was a more hopeless enterprise undertaken, in ordinary circumstances, than that of convicting a smuggler, unless captured *in flagrante delicto*.

CHAPTER VII

OUTRAGE AT HASTINGS BY THE RUXLEY GANG—BATTLE ON THE WHITSTABLE-CANTERBURY ROAD—CHURCH-TOWERS AS SMUGGLERS' CELLARS—THE DRUMMER OF HURSTMONCEUX—EPITAPH AT TANDRIDGE—DEPLORABLE AFFAIR AT HASTINGS—A SHOOTING AFFRAY AND ITS SEQUEL—THE INCIDENT OF "THE FOUR BROTHERS"

SUSSEX was again the scene of a barbarous incident, in 1768; and on this occasion seafaring men were the malefactors.

It is still an article of faith with the writers of guide-books who do not make their own inquiries, and thus perpetuate obsolete things, that to call a Hastings fisherman a "Chop-back" will rouse him to fury. But when a modern visitor, primed with such romance as this, timidly approaches one of these broad-shouldered and amply-paunched fisherfolk and suggests "Chop-backs" as a subject of inquiry, I give you my word they only look upon you with a puzzled expression, and don't understand in the least your meaning.

But in an earlier generation this was a term of great offence to the Hastingers. It arose, according to tradition, from the supposed descent of these fisherfolk from the Norse rovers who used the axe, and cleaved their enemies with them from skull to chine. But the true facts of the case are laid to the account of some of the notorious Ruxley gang, who in 1768 boarded a Dutch hoy, the *Three Sisters*, in mid-channel, on pretence of trading, and chopped

THE RUXLEY GANG

the master, Peter Bootes, down the back with a hatchet. This horrid deed might never have come to light had not these ruffians betrayed themselves by bragging to one another of their cleverness, and dwelling upon the way in which the Dutchman wriggled when they had slashed him on the backbone.

The Government in November of that year sent a detachment of two hundred Inniskilling Dragoons to Hastings to arrest the men implicated, and a man-o'-war and cutter lay off shore to receive them when they had been taken prisoners. The soldiers had strict orders to keep their mission secret, but the day after their arrival they were called out to arrest rioters who had violently assaulted the Mayor, whom they suspected of laying information against the murderers. The secret of the reason for the soldiers' coming had evidently in some manner leaked out. Several arrests of rioters were made, and the men implicated in the outrage on the Dutch boat were duly taken into custody.

The whole affair was so closely interwoven with smuggling that it was by many suspected that the men who had been seized were held for that offence as well; and persons in the higher walks of the smuggling business, namely, those who financed it, and those others who largely purchased the goods, grew seriously alarmed for their own liberty. In the panic that thus laid hold of the town a well-to-do shopkeeper absconded altogether.

Thirteen men were indicted in the Admiralty Court on October 30th, 1769, for piracy and murder on the high seas; namely, Thomas Phillips, elder and younger, William and George Phillips, Mark Chatfield, Robert Webb, Thomas and Samuel Ailsbury, James and Richard Hyde, William Geary, *alias*

Justice, *alias* George Wood, Thomas Knight, and William Wenham, and were capitally convicted. Of these, four, Thomas Ailsbury, William Geary, William Wenham, and Richard Hyde, were hanged at Execution Dock, November 27th.

The next most outstanding incident, a bloody affray which occurred on February 26th, 1780, belongs to Kent.

As Mr. Joseph Nicholson, supervisor of excise, was removing to Canterbury a large seizure of geneva he had made at Whitstable, a numerous body of smugglers followed him and his escort of a corporal and eight troopers of the 4th Dragoons. Fifty of the smugglers had fire-arms, and, coming up with the escort, opened fire without warning or demanding their goods. Two Dragoons were killed on the spot, and two others dangerously wounded. The smugglers then loaded up the goods and disappeared. A reward of £100 was at once offered by the Commissioners of Excise, with a pardon, for informers; and Lieutenant-Colonel Hugonin, of the 4th Dragoons, offered another £50. John Knight, of Whitstable, was shortly afterwards arrested, on information received, and was tried and convicted at Maidstone Assizes. He was hanged on Penenden Heath and his body afterwards gibbeted on Borstal Hill, the spot where the attack had been made.

The south held unquestioned pre-eminence, as long as smuggling activities lasted, and the records of bloodshed and hard-fought encounters are fullest along the coasts of Kent and Sussex. Sometimes, but not often, they are varied by a touch of humour.

The convenience afforded by churches for the

THE CHURCH OF HOVE

storing of smuggled goods is a commonplace of the history of smuggling; and there is scarce a seaboard church of which some like tale is not told, while not a few inland church-towers and churchyards enjoy the same reputation. Asked to account for this almost universal choice of a hiding-place by the smugglers, a parish clerk of that age supposed, truly enough, that it was because no one was ever likely to go near a church, except on Sundays. This casts an instructive side-light upon the Church of England and religion at any time from two hundred to seventy or eighty years ago.

But a tale of more than common humour was told of the old church at Hove, near Brighton, many years ago. It seems that this ancient building had been greatly injured by fire in the middle of the seventeenth century, but that the population was so small and so little disposed to increase that a mere patching up of the ruins was sufficient for local needs. Moreover, the spiritual needs of the place were considered to be so small that Hove and Preston parishes were ecclesiastically united, and were served by one clergyman, who conducted service at each parish church on alternate Sundays. At a later period, indeed, Hove church was used only once in six weeks.

But in the alternate Sunday period the smugglers of this then lonely shore found the half-ruined church of Hove peculiarly useful for their trade; hence the following story.

One "Hove Sunday" the vicar, duly robed, appeared here to take the duty, and found, greatly to his surprise, that no bell was ringing to call the faithful to worship. "Why is the bell not ringing?" demanded the vicar.

"Preston Sunday, sir," returned the sexton shortly.

"No, no," replied the vicar.

"Indeed, then, sir, 'tis."

But the vicar was not to be argued out of his own plain conviction that he had taken Preston last Sunday, and desired the sexton to start the bell-ringing at once.

"'Tain't no good, then, sir," said the sexton, beaten back into his last ditch of defence: "you can't preach to-day."

"*Can't*, fellow?" angrily responded the vicar; "what do you mean by 'can't'?"

"Well, then, sir," said the sexton, "if you must know, the church is full of tubs, and the pulpit's full of tea."

An especially impudent smuggling incident was reported from Hove on Sunday, October 16th, 1819, in the following words:

"A suspected smuggling boat being seen off Hove by some of the custom-house officers, they, with two of the crew of the *Hound* revenue cutter, gave chase in a galley. On coming up with the boat their suspicions were confirmed, and they at once boarded her; but while intent on securing their prize, nine of the smugglers leapt into the *Hound's* galley and escaped. Landing at Hove, seven of them got away at once, two being taken prisoners by some officers who were waiting for them. Upon this a large company of smugglers assembled, at once commenced a desperate attack upon the officers, and, having overpowered them, assaulted them with stones and large sticks, knocked them down, and cut the belts of the chief officer's arms, which they took away, and thereby enabled the two prisoners to escape."

THE DRUMMER OF HURSTMONCEUX

HURSTMONCEUX

A reward of £200 was offered, but without result. The cargo of the smugglers consisted of 225 tubs of gin, 52 tubs of brandy, and one bag of tobacco.

Many of the ghost stories of a hundred years and more ago originated in the smugglers' midnight escapades. It was, of course, entirely to their advantage that superstitious people who heard unaccountable sounds and saw indescribable sights should go off with the notion that supernatural beings were about, and resolve thenceforward to go those haunted ways no more. The mysterious "ghostly drummer" of Hurstmonceux, who was often heard and seen by terrified rustics whose way led them past the ruined castle at night, was a confederate of the Hastings and Eastbourne smugglers, to whom those roofless walls and the hoary tombs of the adjoining churchyard were valuable storehouses. Rubbed with a little phosphorus, and parading those spots once in a way with his drum, they soon became shunned. The tombstones in Hurstmonceux churchyard, mostly of the kind known as "altar-tombs," had slabs which the smugglers easily made to turn on swivels; and from them issued at times spirits indeed, but not such as would frighten many men. The haunted character of Hurstmonceux ceased with the establishment of the coastguard in 1831, and the drummer was heard to drum no more.

The churchyards of the Sussex coast and its neighbourhood still bear witness to the fatal affrays between excisemen and smugglers that marked those times; and even far inland may be found epitaphs on those who fell, breathing curses and Divine vengeance on the persons who brought them to an untimely end. Thus at Tandridge, Surrey, near Godstone, may be seen a tall tombstone beside the south porch of the church, to one Thomas Todman, aged thirty-one years, who was shot dead in a smuggling affray in 1781. Opposite are the lamentable verses, oddities of grammar, spelling, and punctuation duly preserved. The prudery of some conscientious objector to the word "wretch" has caused it to be almost obliterated.

At Patcham, near Brighton, the weatherworn epitaph on the north side of the church to Daniel Scales may still with difficulty be deciphered :

> Sacred to the memory of DANIEL SCALES
> who was unfortunately shot on Thursday evening,
> November 7th 1796.
>
> Alas! swift flew the fatal lead,
> Which piercèd through the young man's head
> He instant fell, resigned his breath,
> And closed his languid eyes in death.
> All you who do this stone draw near,
> Oh! pray let fall the pitying tear.
> From this sad instance may we all,
> Prepare to meet Jehovah's call.

Daniel Scales was one of a desperate smuggling gang, who had had many narrow escapes, but was at last shot through the head.

Again, at Westfield, Sussex, not far from Rye, may be found an old stone, rapidly going to decay, bearing some lines to the memory of a smuggler named Moon :

> In memory of JOHN MOON,
> who was deprived of life by a base man, on the 20th of June 1809,
> in the 28th year of his age.
>
> 'Tis mine to-day to moulder in the earth. . . .

The rest is not now readable.

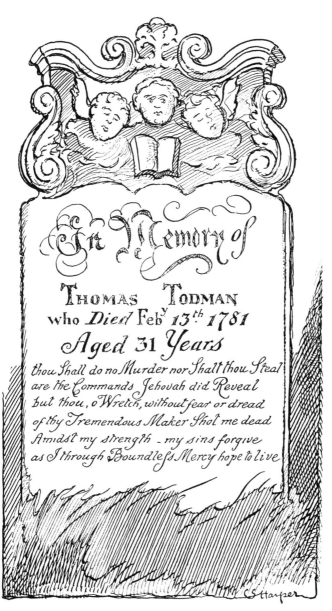

EPITAPH TO THOMAS TODMAN AT TANDRIDGE

THE COAST BLOCKADE

With the close of the Napoleonic wars it was found that smuggling at once immensely increased, for all sorts of reasons; among them the great numbers of men, now unemployed, who had been engaged in naval and military operations, and were reckless and daring fellows, not averse from a life of adventure. The seamen class were the greatest sufferers on the return of peace, nearly 150,000 having been employed in the Navy. In May, 1816, it was reported that 5,000 had emigrated to America, and that large numbers were destitute at home. A Treasury minute of this time truly declared, " They will be the ready instruments of those desperate persons who have a little capital and are hardy enough to engage in the traffic of smuggling."

The Preventive service, long in operation, had, in point of fact, through the ill-support of the Government and the small establishment maintained, been rather a provocation than a prevention; for, as we have seen, while it had not force enough to suppress smuggling, the efforts of its zealous officers to do so brought about murderous conflicts and solitary assassinations on the part of men determined not to lose their goods.

The Coast Blockade, made possible by the ships of the Navy being now not required against a foreign foe, was established in 1816, but it began by being merely nominal and was not immediately supported by a force ashore. It comprised the coasts of Kent and Sussex, from Stangate Creek, near Rochester, to Portsmouth, and was eventually extended to the Hampshire and Dorset coasts.

When it was seen that patrolling ships were not a sufficient deterrent against smugglers who were shore-going as well as seafaring, the Coast Blockade service became equally amphibious, and included parties of seamen, under their own officers—lieutenants and midshipmen—distributed along the shore.

That the old-time prejudice against Government officials in general, and Preventive-men in particular, was as strong amongst the Hastings people during the early years of the nineteenth century as in the days, so graphically described, some sixty years earlier, by the Surveyor-General, Mr. Collier, will be evident from what is about to be related.

Almost immediately after the Coast Blockade had been established, the Solicitor to the Admiralty wrote to Captain McCulloch, that in consequence of a man belonging to Hastings, called Baker, having been killed by a shot from the Revenue cutter *Grecian*, it had come to his knowledge that the Hastings smugglers had expressed their intention of killing as many of the *Grecian's* crew as they could, in revenge. The information had been obtained through an old smuggler called Bowyer, who had been taken out of his wherry at Spithead and sent on board the *Queen Charlotte;* and he had been told by his son, who had helped to carry Baker's body on board the *Market Maid*, of Hastings. This information had been imparted to the Solicitor under promise of secrecy as to its source, as the son's life would not be safe if the source of information were disclosed. Baker had been buried at Haslar Hospital. The official communication is dated Portsmouth, June 6th, 1816.

The bitter feeling thus created was intensified five years later (1821) by the shooting of a fisherman called Swain, on the beach at Hastings, which

AFFRAY AT HASTINGS

occurred, an officer tells us, in the following manner :
"At Hastings, where a fleet of sixty fishing-boats often landed in a single tide, it was impossible to undergo the labour of pulling out and re-stowing all the heavy nets, although it was well known that smuggled goods were very frequently concealed underneath. The Blockade sentinels were therefore furnished with sharp iron prickers, to pierce through the nets; but as this could not be done without slightly injuring the meshes, it was generally objected to as unjustifiable by the fishermen. Upon one of these occasions a man named England proceeded to examine the boat of Joseph Swain, who declared that he would not permit his nets to be injured by the pricker; and as England persevered, a scuffle ensued, in which the latter was struck and thrown out upon the beach. Irritated at this rough usage, he drew forth his pistol, and shot poor Swain dead upon the spot. The sensation this event caused in Hastings will not easily be forgotten. A furious mob surrounded the prisoner, and England would probably have been dragged forth to instant death, if a military guard had not been employed to intimidate the populace."

If this was the story that obtained currency at Hastings, it is no wonder that the mob tried to lynch England. But is it the true version? One would suppose that a naval officer, of long service and experience, himself a member of the force whose credit was at stake—though not a witness of the episode—would be sure of his facts before committing such a story to print. And doubtless it was under this belief that the industrious penmen who provide sensational matter for the delectation of too credulous youth have made such free use of the above " yarn " in their compilations. Researches undertaken place the matter in a very different light; and as in this instance the trite saying "truth is stranger than fiction " once more holds good, there can be no hesitation in placing the facts before the reader.

Lieutenant Mark Sweeny, a cool and reliable officer, who was in command of the Hastings Blockade, in reporting the affair to his superior, thus describes it : " England got into the fishing-boat (as look-out-man, to search), the deceased resisted, striking him and throwing him out of the boat, and following him and repeating the blow, and forcing the cutlass out of his hand, flung it into the sea : he then attempted to take from him his pistol, in which act he lost his life." The bullet passed through the unfortunate man's body into the fleshy part of the arm.

Lieutenant Sweeny then goes on to state : " England has been given over to the civil authorities. By timely aid given by parties from Priory, Ecclesbourne, and Nos. 39, 42, 44, and 45 Towers, we were enabled to overawe the infuriated populace, in which we were aided promptly by the cavalry stationed here and at Bexhill.

" After the ferment had somewhat subsided," he continues, " the party at Hastings Watch-house went to the stores for provisions, and were assailed with missiles, so furiously as to put them in imminent danger of their lives, and one of them, after receiving three or four contusions, fired his pistol without doing any execution; he, also, has been given up at the requisition of a Magistrate, and, with England, is now lodged in the Hastings Gaol." And he proceeds to explain the dangerous situation : " The

EXCITEMENT AT HASTINGS 127

inhabitants threaten us with vengeance, and I much fear, that without the most active interference of the magistrates many lives will be lost. . . . The feeling of indignation and revenge, so strongly manifested by the Hastings smugglers, is directed against Mr. George, for the rigid manner in which he discharges his duty, particularly in having the fishing-boats so closely examined.

"Persons, from humane motives, have, in the course of this evening, informed him that his murder is resolved on, and it is therefore considered advisable to have him removed, as the only way to ensure his personal safety and to appease the perturbed feeling; to which I cannot assent, being of opinion that it would encourage a spirit of opposition, hitherto unknown, under the impression that it would deter his successor from an equally praiseworthy performance of his duty. At the same time, continuing him here after being apprized of the danger to which he is exposed might subject me, besides great disquietude of mind, to the reproach of being accessory to his murder. So circumstanced, I feel how much I stand in need of your instructions, and, if your multifarious duties and health would admit, of your presence."

The situation thus described by Lieutenant Sweeny supplies a striking illustration of the heavy responsibility devolving at times on young naval officers employed on Blockade duties. For there was no friendly telegraph office to run to in those days. The civil authorities were usually indifferent —if not hostile. Legal assistance was, in most instances, unprocurable—the sympathies of the local attorneys being invariably enlisted, by some occult process, on the side of the law-breakers. And thus, cut off from their superiors, to whom, alone, they could look for advice or assistance, at grave crises, when the slightest false move would place them at the mercy of implacable and vengeful foes, the lot of a young Blockade officer was not, it must be conceded, an enviable one.

The man England, having been handed over, as related, to the civil authorities was, after inquiry, committed for trial at the next Assizes, on a charge of wilful murder.

The trial, which caused immense excitement throughout the county of Sussex, was held at Horsham, March 28th, 1821, amidst a crowded Court. The witnesses for the prosecution, nine in number, all of the labouring or seafaring class, came from Hastings, and their evidence went to show that there was a scuffle, and that England, on regaining possession of his pistol, deliberately—so they declared—walked round till he got a clear view of Swain, and then shot him through the body; the pistol, at the time it was fired, being scarcely six inches from Swain.

It came out in Court that although several of the Blockade-men had been examined before the coroner, none of them were called by the prosecution, nor had their depositions been returned. It was further elicited that the coroner's clerk was the attorney for the prosecution. "These circumstances," observed a contemporary, "called forth the strong animadversions of Counsel for the prisoner, and of the Lord Chief Baron."

Five of the Blockade-men were then examined on prisoner's behalf, and their evidence all tended to show that the discharge of the pistol was purely accidental, arising from the suddenness of its release from the grasp of deceased, which caused the prisoner to stagger, and at that moment the pistol went off. They denied that the prisoner took aim, or that he walked round to get a clear shot at the deceased. They declared, further, that both the men were in a violent passion at the time, and that the shooting was an accidental transaction of the moment.

The prisoner, who "appeared to labour under great anxiety during the trial," put in a written defence, in which, after recapitulating the circumstances under which the scuffle took place, earnestly declared that his pistol went off in the suddenness of his separation from the deceased, when released from his hold, and not from any design or premeditation.

In the course of his summing-up, "The Judge," wrote an officer who was present, "pronounced England's conduct to be perfectly justifiable; yet so virulent was the rancour against him, that the jury differed from the Judge, and found the prisoner 'Guilty of wilful murder,' both on the indictment and the Coroner's inquisition."

A painful scene ensued. "The prisoner," we are told, "was greatly agitated on hearing the verdict, and burst into violent grief."

The Lord Chief Baron then addressed him: "George England, a verdict of guilty has been passed against you, and it is my duty to pronounce the sentence of the law, which I cannot avoid; but I have no difficulty, in the face of the country, in saying, that I should have been glad if the verdict had been the other way. At present, however, I must pass the sentence of the law" (Prisoner: "My Lord, have mercy upon me!"), "which is— 'That you be taken from hence'" (Prisoner:

"Consider, I was in the execution of my duty ") "'to the place whence you came'" (Prisoner: "Gentlemen of the jury, pray consider your verdict again "), "'and from thence to the place of execution, on Friday next, where you are to be hanged by the neck until you are dead; and may the Lord have mercy on your soul.'" (Prisoner: "Oh! gentlemen of the jury, pray consider your verdict again!") The Lord Chief Baron: "Prisoner, I'll do all in my power to save your life." (Prisoner: "Do, if you please, my Lord.") The prisoner was then taken from the bar.

The sympathies of the audience were but too plainly indicated at this stage, by several spectators exclaiming, "What! is he not to be hanged after all?"

The Hastings smugglers, as may be supposed, were highly elated over the verdict. Their triumph, however, was short-lived. England was granted an immediate free pardon, and, for his greater security, a discharge from further employment in the Blockade service.

Of England's subsequent career nothing is known. Of one thing we may be sure—that he shook the dust of Hastings, right joyfully, from his feet.

And now, by way of completing this picture of a Sussex watering-place in the year 1821, we must take the reader back to the scene of the trouble. It will be remembered that Lieutenant Sweeny wrote off, hurriedly, for Captain McCulloch. This officer, immediately on receipt of the letter, repaired to Hastings, and, as soon as the excitement had calmed down, proceeded to hold an inquiry, with the object, not only of pouring oil on the troubled waters, but of removing, as far as possible, the particular

CAPTAIN McCULLOCH

grievance which had raised the storm. To this end, Captain McCulloch received deputations from the fishermen, held conferences with the Mayor and magistrates, and made every endeavour to conciliate the infuriated populace.

The chief aim was to so arrange the searching of the boats as to reduce the points of friction to a minimum. A brief experience of the temper of the Hastings people, however, made it clear to Captain McCulloch that he had essayed a hopeless task. What they wanted was to get rid of the Blockademen altogether, and their frame of mind was clearly indicated in the correspondence which ensued between the officer above-named and the authorities in London. From this we learn that, by way of removing the chief grievance, " the needless delay to which the boats were subjected on returning from sea," Captain McCulloch gave orders for six men to be told off for this duty. Whereupon " the fishermen complained of the large number of men employed in searching their boats "; " showing," as the officer justly observed, " how unreasonable they are." And so matters dragged on, proving the correctness of Captain McCulloch's comment on the whole proceedings, " that the fishermen merely wanted an excuse for continuing their illicit practices." In short, the Hastings men had changed but little since the time (1749) when the Surveyor-General's clerk declared that " nine parts in ten of the populace would as freely murder a man who had excited their enmity as they would eat or drink when hungry or dry."

The inquirer who would seek out a person in Hastings, at the present day, with any recollection of this once-famous affair—or, indeed, who had ever heard of it—would have to travel far. There remains, however, a solemn reminder of it, in the form of a headstone, which stands, unnoticed by passers-by, in the south-east corner of All Saints' Churchyard, bearing the following inscription:

> This Stone
> Sacred to the memory of
> Joseph Swain Fisherman
> was erected at the expence of
> the members of the friendly
> Society of Hastings.

In commiseration of his cruel and untimely death, and as a record of the public indignation at the needlefs and sanguinary violence of which he was the unoffending Victim.

He was shot by Geo. England, one of the Sailors employ'd in the Coast blockade service, in open day, on the 13th March, 1821, and almost instantly expir'd, in the twenty-ninth Year of his age, leaving a Widow and five small children to lament his lofs.

A search amongst some files of old Sussex newspapers brought the following curious paragraph to light: "Hastings, Jan. 9th, 1832. The widow of a man shot by Preventive-men in 1821, had her house broken into, and a pair of pantaloons belonging to her husband stolen, containing money which had been there since his death."

That the Hastings smugglers were not, all, the bloodthirsty villains that might be supposed from the antecedents of the place is shown by an episode related by Lieutenant Chappell. He tells us that one of the most noted of the local fraternity was a fat, good-natured fellow called Raper, who commanded a remarkably fast-sailing lugger, called the *Little Anne*. Though an inveterate free-trader, so far from assailing the "Warriors" with taunts and abuse, like the rest of his comrades, Raper conducted himself with undeviating civility. On being asked

THE 'FOUR BROTHERS'

by an officer, once, why he did not quit smuggling and turn fisherman, he replied " What! would you have me sit bobbing an eel all day, to catch sixpen'orth of whiting? No! I was born a smuggler, I was bred a smuggler, and I shall die a smuggler; but I have no wish to see my children tread in the same footsteps. If either of my boys gets into a boat, I'll either break his legs or make him a linendraper, sooner than he shall larn all the trouble that his father has experienced."

The affair of the *Badger* revenue cutter and the *Four Brothers* smuggling lugger was the next exciting event. It happened on January 13th, 1823, and attracted a great deal of attention at the time, not only on account of the severe encounter at sea, but from the subsequent trial of the crew of the smuggler. The *Four Brothers* was a Folkestone boat, and her crew of twenty-six were chiefly Folkestone men. She was a considerable vessel, having once been a French privateer, and was, as a privateer had need to be, a smart, easily handled craft, capable of giving the go-by to most other vessels. She carried four six-pound carronades. In constant commission, her crew pouched a pound a week wages, with an additional ten guineas for each successful run.

On January 12th, of this momentous voyage, she sailed from Flushing with over one hundred tons of leaf-tobacco aboard, snugly packed for convenience of carriage in bales of 60 lb., and carried also a small consignment of brandy and gin, contained in 50 half-ankers, and 13 chests of tea—all destined for the south of Ireland. Ship and cargo were worth some £11,000; so it is sufficiently evident that her owners were in a considerable way of business of the contraband kind.

At daybreak on the morning of January 13th, when off Dieppe and sailing very slowly, in a light wind, the crew of the *Four Brothers* found themselves almost upon what they at first took to be French fishing-boats, and held unsuspiciously on her course. Suddenly, however, one of them ran a flag smartly up her halliards and fired a gun across the bows of the *Four Brothers*, as a signal to bring her to. It was the revenue cutter *Badger*.

Unfortunately for the smuggler, she was carrying a newly stepped mainmast, and under small sail only, and accordingly, in disobeying the summons and attempting to get away, she was speedily outsailed.

The smuggler, unable to get away, hoisted the Dutch colours and opened the fight that took place by firing upon the *Badger*, which immediately returned it. For two hours this exchange of shots was maintained. Early in the encounter William Cullum, seaman, was killed aboard the *Badger*, and Lieutenant Nazer, in command, received a shot from a musket in the left shoulder. One man of the *Four Brothers* was killed outright, and nine wounded, but the fight would have continued had not the *Badger* sailed into the starboard quarter of the smuggler, driving her bowsprit clean through her adversary's mainsail. Even then the smuggler's crew endeavoured to fire one of her guns, but failed.

The commander of the *Badger* thereupon called upon the *Four Brothers* to surrender; or, according to his own version, the smugglers themselves called for quarter; and the mate and some of the cutter's men went in a boat and received their submission,

THE 'FOUR BROTHERS' 135

and sent them prisoners aboard the *Badger*. The smugglers claimed that they had surrendered only on condition that they should have their boats and personal belongings and be allowed to go ashore; but it seems scarce likely the Lieutenant could have promised so much. The *Four Brothers* was then taken into Dover Harbour and her crew sent aboard the *Severn* man-o'-war and kept in irons in the cockpit. Three of her wounded died there. The others, after a short interval, were again put aboard the *Badger* and taken up the Thames to imprisonment on the Tower tender for a further three or four days. Thence they were removed, all handcuffed and chained, in a barge and committed to the King's Bench Prison. At Bow Street, on the following day, they were all formally committed for trial, and then remitted to the King's Bench Prison for eleven weeks, before the case came on.

On Friday, April 25th, 1823, the twenty-two prisoners were arraigned in the High Court of Admiralty; Marinel Krans, master of the *Four Brothers*, and his crew, nearly all of whom bore Dutch names, being charged with wilfully and feloniously firing on the revenue cutter *Badger*, on January 13th, 1823, on the high seas, about eight miles off Dungeness, within the jurisdiction of the High Court of Admiralty of England.

Mr. Brougham, afterwards Lord Brougham, defended, the defence being that the *Four Brothers* was a Dutch vessel, owned at Flushing, and her crew Dutchmen. A great deal of very hard swearing went towards this ingenious defence, for the crew, it is hardly necessary to say, were almost all English. At least one witness for the prosecution was afraid to appear in consequence of threats made by prisoners' friends, and an affidavit was put in to that effect. It appeared, in the evidence given by the commander of the *Badger* and other witnesses for the prosecution, that the prisoners all spoke excellent English at the time of the capture, and afterwards; but they, singularly enough, understood little or none when in court, and had to be communicated with through the agency of an interpreter.

In summing-up, Mr. Justice Park said the crime for which the prisoners were tried was not murder, but was a capital offence. Two things, if found by the jury, would suffice to acquit the prisoners. The first was that no part of the vessel which they navigated belonged to any subject of His Majesty; the other that one half of the crew were not His Majesty's subjects. For if neither of these facts existed, His Majesty's ship had no right to fire at their vessel. But if the jury believed that any part of the vessel was British property, or that one half of her crew were British subjects, then His Majesty's ship *Badger*, under the circumstances that had been proved, being on her duty, and having her proper colours flying, was justified in boarding their vessel; and their making resistance by firing at the *Badger* was a capital offence. The reason for the evidence respecting the distance of the vessels from the French coast being given was that, by the law of nations, ships of war were not, in time of peace, permitted to molest any vessel within one league of the coast of any other Power.

The jury, after deliberating for two hours, returned a verdict of "Not Guilty" for all the prisoners, finding that the ship and cargo were wholly foreign property, and that more than one half the crew were foreigners. They were, accordingly, at once liberated, and returned to Folkestone in midst of great popular rejoicings. The *Four Brothers* was also released, and the commander of the *Badger* had the mortification of being obliged to escort her out of Dover harbour.

Dover town was, about this time, the scene of stirring events. One Lieutenant Lilburn, in command of a revenue cutter, had captured a smuggler, and had placed the crew in Dover gaol. As they had not offered armed resistance to the capture, their offence was not capital, but they were liable to service on board a man-o'-war—a fate they were most anxious to avoid. These imprisoned men were largely natives of Folkestone and Sandgate, and their relatives determined to march over the ten miles between those places and Dover, and, if possible, liberate them. When they arrived in Dover, and their intention became known, a crowd of fisherfolk and longshore people swarmed out of the Dover alley-ways and reinforced them. Prominent among them were the women, who, as ever in cases of popular tumult, proved themselves the most violent and destructive among the mob. Nothing less than the destruction of the gaol was decided upon, and the more active spirits, leaving others to batter in the walls, doors, and windows, climbed upon the roof, and from that vantage-point showered bricks and tiles upon the Mayor and the soldiers who had been called out. The Mayor, beset with tooth and claw by screeching women, who tore the Riot Act out of his hand, fled, and Lieutenant Lilburn exhorted the officer in charge of the military to fire upon the crowd, but he declined; and meanwhile the tradespeople and respectable inhabitants busied themselves in barricading their shops and houses.

The prisoners were triumphantly liberated, taken to a blacksmith's, where their irons were knocked off, and then driven off in postchaises to Folkestone, whence they dispersed to their several hiding-places.

CHAPTER VIII

FATAL AFFRAYS AND DARING ENCOUNTERS AT RYE, DYMCHURCH, EASTBOURNE, BO-PEEP, AND FAIRLIGHT—THE SMUGGLERS' ROUTE FROM SHOREHAM AND WORTHING INTO SURREY—THE MILLER'S TOMB—LANGSTON HARBOUR

THE twenties of the nineteenth century formed a period especially rich in smuggling incidents, or perhaps seem so to do, because, with the growth of country newspapers, they were more fully reported, instead of being left merely the subject of local legend.

A desperate affray took place in Rye Harbour so late as May 1826, when a ten-oared smuggling galley, chased by a revenue guard-boat, ran ashore. The smugglers, abandoning their oars, opened fire upon the guard, but the blockade-men from the watch-house at Camber then arrived upon the scene and seized one of the smugglers; whereupon a gang of not fewer than two hundred armed smugglers, who had until that moment been acting as a concealed reserve, rushed violently from behind the sandhills, and commenced firing on the blockade-men, killing one and wounding another. They were, however, ultimately driven off, with the capture of their galley, but managed to carry off their wounded.

On another occasion, four or five smugglers were drowned whilst swimming the Military

Canal, with tubs slung on their backs. They had, in the dark, missed the spot where it was fordable. Romney Marsh, and the wide-spreading levels of Pett, Camber, Guilford, and Dunge Marsh had—as we have already seen, in the account of the owlers given in earlier pages— ever been the smugglers' Alsatia.

The Rev. Richard Harris Barham, author of the *Ingoldsby Legends*, has placed upon record some of his meetings with smugglers in "this recondite region," as he was pleased to style it; and his son, in the life he wrote of his father, adds to them. Barham, ordained in 1813, and given the curacy of Westwell, near Ashford, had not long to wait before being brought into touch with the lawless doings here. One of the desperate smugglers of the Marsh had been shot through the body in an encounter with the riding-officers, and fatally wounded. As he lay dying, Barham was brought to convey to him the last consolations of religion, and was startled when the smuggler declared there was no crime of which he had not been guilty.

"Murder is not to be reckoned among them, I hope," exclaimed the not easily shocked clergyman.

"Too many of them!" was the startling response of the dying man.

In 1817 Barham was collated by the Archbishop of Canterbury to the adjoining livings of Warehorne and Snargate, the first-named situated on the verge of the marsh; the second situated, moist and forbidding, in the marsh itself. The winding road between these two villages crossed the then newly made Royal Military Canal by

DYMCHURCH

a bridge. Often, as the clergyman was returning, late at night, to his comfortable parsonage at Warehorne, he was met and stopped by some mysterious horsemen; but when he mentioned his name he was invariably allowed to proceed, and, as he did so, a long and silent company of mounted smugglers defiled past, each man with his led horse laden with tubs. The grey tower of Snargate church he frequently found, by the aroma of tobacco it often exhaled, instead of its customary and natural mustiness, to have been recently used as a store for smuggled bales of that highly taxed article.

The *Cinque Ports Herald* of 1826 records the landing on a night in May, or in the early hours of the morning, of a considerable cargo of contraband hereabouts:

"A large party of smugglers had assembled in the neighbourhood of Dymchurch, and a boat laden (as is supposed) with tubs of spirits, being observed to approach the shore nearly opposite to Dymchurch, the smugglers instantly commenced cheering, and rushed upon the coast, threatening defiance to the sentinels of the Blockade; who, perceiving such an overwhelming force, gave the alarm, when a party of marines, coming to their assistance, a general firing took place. The smugglers retreated into the marshes, followed by the blockade-men, and, from their knowledge of the ground, were indebted for their ultimate escape. We regret to state two of the Blockade seamen were wounded; one severely in the arm, which must cause amputation, and the other in the face, by slug shots. There can be no doubt but that some of the smugglers must have been wounded, if not killed. One of their muskets was picked up loaded—abandoned, no doubt, by the bearer of it, on account of wounds. The boat, with her cargo, was obliged to put to sea again, without effecting a landing, and, notwithstanding the vigilance of Lieutenants Westbrook, Mudge, and McLeod, who were afloat in their galleys on the spot, from the darkness of the night, effected its escape. We have also heard that a run of five hundred tubs took place on the Sussex coast last week, not far from Hastings, the smugglers losing only eleven tubs. This was also effected by force, and with such a superiority in number that they completely overpowered the Blockade force."

The *Brighton Gazette*, of a few days later, contained the following :

" We have been favoured with some particulars of another recent attempt to work contraband goods a few miles eastward of Eastbourne, when it appears the Coast Blockade succeeded in taking a large boat and upwards of two hundred tubs. We are sorry to add much mischief has occurred, as on the following morning blood was observed near the spot. Two men, it is said, belonging to the boat are taken prisoners, and two of the Blockade are reported to be much bruised and beaten, and it is also suspected some of the smugglers are seriously, if not mortally, wounded. The Blockade in this instance behaved in the most humane manner, having received a regular volley from their opponents before their officers gave directions for them to fire. We have just heard that five smugglers were killed in the affray."

A LANDING AT BO-PEEP

BO-PEEP

On a Sunday night towards the end of July 1826, during a run of smuggled goods at Dover, the smugglers shot dead a seaman of the preventive force named Morgan, for which no one was ever convicted.

A determined and blood-stained struggle took place at Bo-Peep at midnight of January 3rd, 1828. Bo-Peep was the name of a desolate spot situated midway between Hastings and Bexhill. The place is the same as that westernmost extension of St. Leonards now known by the eminently respectable—not to say imposing—name of "West Marina"; but in those times it was a shore, not indeed lonely (better for its reputation had it been so) but marked by an evil-looking inn, to which were attached still more evil-looking "Pleasure Gardens." If throats were not, in fact, commonly cut in those times at Bo-Peep, the inn and its deplorable "Pleasure Gardens" certainly looked no fit, or safe, resort for any innocent young man with a pocketful of money jingling as he walked.

On this occasion a lugger came in view off shore, when a party of smugglers armed, as usual, with "bats," *i. e.* stout ash-poles, some six feet in length, rushed to the beach, landed the cargo, and made off with it, by various means, inland a distance of some three miles to Sidley Green. Here the Coast Blockade-men, some forty in number, came up with them.

The smugglers drew up in regular line-formation and a desperate fight resulted. The smugglers fought with such determination and courage that the Blockade-men were repulsed and one, Quartermaster Collins, was killed. In the first volley fired by the Blockade an old smuggler named Smithurst was killed; his body was found next morning, with his "bat" still grasped in his hand, the stout staff almost hacked to pieces by the cutlasses and bayonets of the Blockade-men.

At the Spring Assizes held at Horsham, Spencer Whiteman, of Udimore, Thomas Miller, Henry Miller, John Spray, Edward Shoesmith, William Bennett, John Ford, and Stephen Stubberfield were indicted for assembling, armed, for purposes of smuggling, and were removed for trial to the Old Bailey, where, on April 10th, they all pleaded guilty; as did Whiteman, Thomas Miller, Spray, Bennett, and Ford, together with Thomas Maynard and William Plumb, for a like offence on January 23rd, 1828, at Eastbourne. Sentence of death was passed on all, but was commuted to transportation. With three exceptions, they were young men under thirty years of age.

Again in broad daylight, in 1828, a lugger landed a heavy cargo of kegs on the open beach at Bo-Peep. No fewer than three hundred rustic labourers, who had been hired by the job, in the usual course, by the smugglers bold, assembled on the beach, and formed up two lines of guards while the landing of the tubs, and their loading into carts, on horses, or on men's shoulders, was proceeding. If the preventive officers knew anything of what was toward that busy day they did not, at any rate, interfere; and small blame to them for the very elementary discretion they displayed. They had, as already shown, been too seriously mauled at an earlier date for them to push matters again to extremity.

On January 3rd, 1831, in Fairlight Glen, two

AT CAMBER CASTLE

miles east of Hastings, two smugglers, William Cruttenden and Joseph Harrod, were shot dead. These were the last days of the Coast Blockade. None of the many holiday-makers who now in summer visit this picturesque spot can conceive the conditions then prevailing here, when the picturesque was hardly as yet established.

Still the tale was continued, for during a landing on January 23rd, 1833, at Eastbourne, the smugglers, who had assembled in large numbers, killed George Pett, chief boatman of the local preventive station, and ran their cargo safely. Several of both sides were wounded on this occasion, but no one among the smugglers was ever arrested.

The last fatal happening in this way along the Sussex coast appears to have been in the marshes at Camber Castle, on April 1st, 1838, when a poor fiddler of Winchelsea, named Thomas Monk, was shot in the course of a dispute over run goods by the coastguard.

But we may quite easily have a surfeit of these brutal affrays, and it is better to dwell on a lighter note, to contemplate the audacity, and to admire the ingenuity and the resource often displayed by the smugglers in concealing their movements.

To especially single out any particular line of coast for pre-eminence in smuggling would be impossible. When everyone smuggled, and everyone else—owing to that well-understood human foible of buying in the cheapest market—supported smuggling by purchasing smuggled goods, every foreshore that did not actually present physical difficulties, or that was not exceptionally under excise and customs surveillance, was a free port, in a very special signification. The thickly peopled coast-line of Kent, Sussex, and Hampshire of our own time was then sparsely populated, and those shores that are now but thinly settled were in that age the merest aching wildernesses, where not only towns, but even villages and hamlets, were few and far apart. A coast-line such as that at Brighton would seem to us to present certain obvious difficulties to the smuggler, but close at hand was the low-lying land of Shoreham, with its lagoon-like harbour, a very shy, secretive kind of place to this day; while away to Worthing, and beyond it, stretched a waste of shingle-beach, running up to solitary pasture-lands that reached to the foot of the noble ramparts of the South Downs. On these shores the free-traders landed their illegal imports with little interference, and their shore-going allies received the goods and took them inland, to London or to their intermediate storehouses in the country-side, very much at their leisure. Avoiding the much-travelled high roads, and traversing the chalk-downs by unfrequented bridle-tracks, they went across the level Weald and past the Surrey border into that still lonely district running east and west for many miles, on the line of Leith Hill, Ewhurst, and Hindhead. There, along those wooded heights, whose solitary ways still astonish, with their remote aspect, the Londoner who by any chance comes to them, although but from thirty to thirty-five miles from the Bank of England in the City of London, you may still track, amid the pine-trees on the shoulders of the gorsy hills, or among the oaks that grow so luxuriantly in the Wealden clay, the "soft roads,"

SMUGGLERS' TRACKS NEAR EWHURST

SMUGGLERS' INLAND TRACKS 147

as the country folk call them, along which the smugglers, unmolested, carried their merchandise. On Ewhurst Hill stands a windmill, to which in those times the smugglers' ways converged; and near by, boldly perched on a height, along the sylvan road that leads from Shere to Ewhurst village, stood the "Windmill," once the "New" inn, which had a doubled roof, utilised as a storehouse for clandestine kegs. A "Windmill" inn stands on the spot to-day, but it is a new building, the old house having unfortunately been burned down some some years ago. Surveying the country from this spot, you have, on the one hand, almost precipitous hill-peaks, gorsy to their summits, and on the other a lovely dale, deeply embosomed in woods. The sub-soil here is a soft yellow sandstone, streaked with white sand, breaking out along the often hollow paths into miniature cliffs, in which the smugglers and their allies were not slow to scoop caverns and store part of their stock. We have already learnt how terrible these men could be to those who informed against them or made away with any of their property, and by direct consequence the goods thus stored were generally safe, either from the authorities or from the rustics, who had a very wholesome and well-founded dread of the smuggling bands. But they had a way of their own of letting these justly dreaded folk see that their stores were evident to some, and that silence was supposed to have a certain market value. Their way was just a delicate hint, which consisted in marking a tub or two with a chalk cross; and sure enough, when the stock was removed, those chalk-marked tubs were left behind, with possibly, if the country-folk had been modest and the smugglers were generous, a few others to keep them company.

An old brick-and-tile-hung farm, down below Ewhurst Hill, older than it looks, known as Barhatch, was in those times in possession of the Ticknor family; and still, in what was the old living-room, may be seen the ingle-nook, with its iron crane, marked "John Ticknor, 1755." The Barhatch woods were often used by smugglers, and the Ticknors never had any occasion to purchase spirits, because, at not infrequent intervals, when the household arose, and the front door was opened in the morning, a keg would be found deposited on the steps; a complimentary keg, for the use of the Ticknor property and the discretion of the Ticknor tongue.

One of the choicest landing-places along the Sussex coast must undoubtedly have been just westward of Worthing, by Goring, where the shore is yet secluded, and is even now not readily come at by good roads. In a line with it is Highdown Hill, a rounded hump of the Downs, rising to a height of two hundred and ninety-nine feet, two miles inland; a spot famed in all guide-book lore of this neighbourhood as the site of the "Miller's Tomb." This miller, whose real business of grinding corn seems to have been supplemented by participation on the stern joys of illegal importation, was one John Olliver. His mill was situated on this hill-top: a very remote spot, even now, arrived at only along lanes in which mud and water plentifully await the explorer's cautious foot, and where brambles and intruding twigs currycomb his whiskers, if he have such.

THE MILLER OF HIGHDOWN   149

John Olliver, miller, was an eighteenth-century eccentric, whose morbid fancy for having his coffin made early in life and wheeled under his bed every night, was not satisfied until he had also built himself a tomb on the hill-top, on a twelve-foot square plot of ground granted him by the landowner, one W. W. Richardson, in 1766: a tomb on which he could with satisfaction look every day. Yet he was not the dull, dispirited man one might for these reasons suppose; and Pennant, in his *Tour in Sussex*, is found saying, " I am told he is a stout, active, cheerful man." And then comes this significant passage. " Besides his proper trade he carries on a very considerable one in smuggled goods." Let us pause a moment to reflect upon the impudent public manner in which John Olliver must have carried on his smuggling activities. To this impudence he added also figures on his house-top, representing a miller filling a sack and a smuggler chased by an exciseman with a drawn sword; after the exciseman coming a woman with a broom, belabouring him about the head. The tomb the miller had built for eventual occupation by his body was in the meanwhile generally occupied by spirits—not the spirits of the dead, but such *eaux de vie* as hollands and cognac; and he himself was not laid here for many years, for he lived to be eighty-four years of age, and died in 1793. He had long been widely known as an eccentric, and thousands came to his funeral on the unconsecrated spot. Here the tomb, of the altar-tomb type, stands to this day, kept in excellent repair, and the lengthy inscriptions repainted; at whose cost and charges I know not. A small grove of trees almost entirely encircles it. At one end is a gruesome little sculpture representing Death, as a skeleton, laying a hand upon an affrighted person, and asking him, "Whither away so fast?" and at the other end are the following lines:

> Why fhould my fancy anyone offend
> Whofe good or ill does not on it depend
> (A generous gift) on which my Tomb doth ftand
> This is the only fpot that I have chofe
> Wherein to take my lafting long repofe
> Here in the drift my body lieth down
> You'll fay it is not confecrated ground,
> I grant ye fame; but where shall we e'er find
> The fpot that e'er can purify the mind?
> Nor to the body any lufter give.
> This more depends on what a life we live
> For when ye trumpet fhall begin to found
> 'Twill not avail where'er ye Body's found.
> Blefsed are they and all who in the Lord the Saviour die
> Their bodief wait Redemption day,
> And fleep in peace where'er they lay.

On the upper slab are a number of texts and highly moral reflections.

As for the Selsey Peninsula, and the district of flat lands and oozy creeks south of Chichester and on to Portsmouth, Nature would seem almost to have constructed the entire surroundings with the especial objects of securing the smugglers and confounding the customs. Here Sussex merges into Hampshire.

Among the many smuggling nooks along the Hampshire coast, Langston Harbour was prominent, forming, as it does, an almost land-locked lagoon, with creeks ramifying toward Portsea Island on one side and Hayling Island on the other. There still stands on a quay by the waterside at Langston the old "Royal Oak" inn, which

THE MILLER'S TOMB

LANGSTON HARBOUR

was a favourite gathering-place of the "free traders" of these parts, neighboured by a ruined windmill of romantic aspect, to which no stories particularly attach, but whose lowering, secretive appearance aptly accentuates the queer reputation of the spot.

The reputation of Langston Harbour was such that an ancient disused brig, the *Griper*, was permanently stationed here, with the coastguard housed aboard, to keep watch upon the very questionable goings and comings of the sailor-folk and fishermen of the locality. And not only these watery folk needed watching, but also the people of Havant and the oyster-fishers of Emsworth.

That sporadic cases of smuggling long continued in these districts, as elsewhere, after the smuggling era was really ended, we may see from one of the annual reports issued by the Commissioners of Customs. The following incident occurred in 1873, and is thus officially described:

"On the top of a bank rising directly from high-water mark in one of the muddy creeks of Southampton Water stands a wooden hut commanding a full view of it, and surrounded by an ill-cultivated garden. There are houses near, but the hut does not belong to them, and appears to have been built for no obvious purpose. An old smuggler was traced to this hut, and from that time, for nearly two months, the place was watched with great precaution, until at midnight, on May 28th, two men employed by us being on watch, a boat was observed coming from a small vessel about a mile from the shore. The boat, containing four men, stopped opposite the hut, landed one man and some bags, while the remainder of the crew took her some two hundred yards off, hauled her up, and then proceeded to the hut. One of our men was instantly dispatched for assistance, while the other remained watching. On his return with three policemen, the whole party went to the hut, where they found two men on watch outside and four inside, asleep, A horse and cart were also found in waiting, the cart having a false bottom. The six men were secured and sent to the police station; a boat was then procured, the vessel whence the men had come was boarded and found to be laden with tobacco and spirits. The result was that the vessel, a smack of about fifteen tons, with eighty-five bales of leaf-tobacco, six boxes of Cavendish, with some cigars and spirits, was seized, and four of the persons concerned in the transaction convicted of the offence."

LANGSTON HARBOUR

CHAPTER IX

EAST COAST SMUGGLING—OUTRAGE AT BECCLES—A COLCHESTER RAID—CANVEY ISLAND—BRADWELL QUAY—THE EAST ANGLIAN "CART GAPS"—A BLAKENEY STORY—TRAGICAL EPITAPH AT HUNSTANTON—THE PEDDAR'S WAY

THE doings of the Kentish and Sussex gangs entirely overshadow the annals of smuggling in other counties; and altogether, to the general reader, those two seaboards and the coasts of Devon and Cornwall stand out as typical scenes. But no part of our shores was immune; although the longer sea-passages to be made elsewhere of course stood greatly in the way of the "free-traders" of those less favoured regions. After Kent and Sussex, the east coast was probably the most favourable for smuggling. The distance across the North Sea might be greater and the passage often rough, but the low, muddy shores and ramifying creeks of Essex and the sandy coastwise warrens of Suffolk, Norfolk, and Lincolnshire, very sparsely inhabited, offered their own peculiar facilities for the shy and secretive trade.

Nor did the East Anglian smugglers display much less ferocity when their interests were threatened, or their goods seized, than was shown by the yokels of those other counties. The stolid, ox-like rustics of the country-side there, as along the margin of the English Channel, were roused to almost incredible acts of brutality which do not seem to have been repeated in the West.

We do not find the hardy seafaring smugglers often behaving with the cold-blooded cruelty displayed, as a usual phenomenon, by the generally unemotional men of ploughed fields and rustic communities who took up the running and carried the goods inland from the water's edge whither those sea-dogs had brought them. In the being of the men who dared tempestuous winds and waves there existed, as a rule, a more sportsmanlike and generous spirit. Something of the traditional heartiness inseparable from sea-life impelled them to give and take without the black blood that seethed evilly in the veins of the landsmen. The seamen, it seemed, realised that smuggling was a risk; something in the nature of any game of skill into which they entered, with the various officers of the law naturally opposed to them; and when either side won, that was incidental to the game, and no enmity followed as the matter of course it was with their shore-going partners.

Perhaps these considerations, as greatly as the difference in racial characters, show us why the landsmugglers of the Home Counties should have been so criminal, while from the Devon and Cornish contrabandists we hear mostly of humorous passages.

At Beccles, in Suffolk, for example, we find the record, in 1744, of an incident that smacks rather of the Hawkhurst type of outrage. Smugglers there pulled a man out of bed, whipped him, tied him naked on a horse, and rode away with their prisoner, who was never again heard of, although a reward of £50 was offered.

Colchester was the scene, on April 16th, 1847,

EAST ANGLIAN DOINGS 155

of as bold an act as the breaking open of the customhouse at Poole. At two o'clock in the morning two men arrived at the quay at Hythe, by Colchester, and, with the story that they were revenue officers come to lodge a seizure of captured goods, asked to be shown the way to the custom-house. They had no sooner been shown it than there followed thirty smugglers, well armed with blunderbusses and pistols, who, with a heavy blacksmith's hammer and a crowbar, broke open the warehouse, in which a large quantity of dutiable goods was stored. They were not molested in their raid, and went off with sixty oil-bags, containing 1,514 lb. of tea that had been seized near Woodbridge Haven. No one dared interfere with them, and by six o'clock that morning they had proceeded as far as Hadleigh, from which point all trace of them was lost.

Canvey Island, in the estuary of the Thames, off Benfleet, with its quaint old Dutch houses, relics of the seventeenth- and eighteenth-century Hollanders who settled there and carried on a more than questionable business, was reputedly a nest of smugglers. The "Lobster Smack," a quaint old weatherboarded inn built just within the old earthen sea-wall for which those Dutchmen were responsible, and standing somewhat below the level of high water, has legends of smuggling that naturally do not lose by age or repetition.

The Blackwater estuary, running up from the Essex Coast to Maldon, offered peculiar facilities for smuggling; and that, perhaps, is why a coastguard vessel is still stationed at Stansgate, halfway along its length, opposite Osea Island. At the mouth of the Blackwater there branch other creeks and estuaries leading past Mersea Island to

Colchester; and here, looking out upon a melancholy sea, and greatly resembling a barn, stands the ancient chapel of St. Peter-upon-the-Wall, situated in one of the most lonely spots conceivable, on what were, ages ago, the ramparts of the Roman station of *Othona*. It has long been used as a barn, and was in smuggling times a frequent rendezvous of the night-birds who waged ceaseless war with the Customs.

Two miles onward, along sea and river-bank, Bradwell Quay is reached, where the " Green Man " inn in these times turns a hospitable face to the wayfarer, but was in the " once upon a time " apt to distrust the casual stranger, for it was a house " ower sib " with the free-traders, and Pewit Island, just off the quay, a desolate islet almost awash, formed an admirable emergency store. The old stone-floored kitchen of the " Green Man," nowadays a cool and refreshing place in which to take a modest quencher on a summer's day, still remains very much what it was of old; and the quaint fireplace round which the sly longshore men of these Essex creeks foregathered on those winter nights when work was before them keeps its old-time pot-racks and hooks.

Among the very numerous accounts of smuggling affrays we may exhume from the musty files of old newspapers, we read of the desperate encounter in which Mr. Toby, Supervisor of Excise, lost an eye in contending with a gang of smugglers at Caister, near Yarmouth, in April 1816; which shows—if we had occasion to show—that the East Anglian could on occasion be as ferocious as the rustics of the south.

The shores of East Anglia we have already noted to be largely composed of wide-spreading, sand

THE "GREEN MAN," BRADWELL QUAY

BLAKENEY

flats, in whose wastes the tracks of wild birds and animals—to say nothing of the deeply indented footmarks of heavily-laden men—are easily distinguished; and the chief problem of the free-traders of those parts was therefore often how to cover up the tracks they left so numerously in their passage across to the hard roads. In this resort the shepherds were their mainstay, and for the usual consideration, *i.e.* a keg of the " right stuff," would presently, after the gang had passed, come driving their flocks along in the sandy trail they had left : completely obliterating all evidences of a run of contraband goods having been successfully brought off.

Blakeney, on the Norfolk coast, is associated with one of the best and most convincing tales ever told of smuggling. This coast is rich in what are known as " cart gaps " : dips in the low cliffs, where horses and carts may readily gain access to the sea. These places were, of course, especially well watched by the preventive men, who often made a rich haul out of the innocent-looking farm-carts, laden with seaweed for manure, that were often to be observed being driven landwards at untimeous hours of night and early morn. Beneath the seaweed were, of course, numerous kegs. Sometimes the preventive men confiscated horses and carts, as well as their loads, and all were put up for sale. On one of these painful occasions the local custom-house officer, who knew a great deal more of the sea and its ways than he did of horses, was completely taken in by a farmer-confederate of the smugglers whose horses had been seized. The farmer went to make an offer for the animals, and was taken to see them. The season of the year was the spring, when, as the poet observes, "a young man's fancy lightly turns to thoughts of love"—and when horses shed their coats. Up went the farmer to the nearest horse, and easily, of course, pulled out a handful of hair. "Why," said he, in the East Anglian way, "th' poor brute surely du fare to hev gotten t' mange, and all o' them tudderuns 'ull ketch it, ef yow bain't keerful." And then he examined "tudderuns," and behold! each *had* caught it: and so he bought the lot for five pounds. That same night every horse was back in its own stable.

Searching in graveyards is not perhaps the most exhilarating of pastimes or employments, but it, at any rate, is likely to bring, on occasion, curious local history to light. Not infrequently, in the old churchyards of seaboard parishes, epitaphs bearing upon the story of smuggling may be found.

Among these often quaint and curious, as well as tragical, relics, that in Hunstanton churchyard, on the coast of Norfolk, is pre-eminent, both for its grotesquely ungrammatical character and for the history that attaches to the affair:

> In Memory of William Webb, late of the 15th Lt. D'ns, who was shot from his Horse by a party of Smugglers on the 26 of Sepr. 1784.
>
> I am not dead, but sleepeth here,
> And when the Trumpet Sound I will appear.
> Four balls thro' me Pearced there way:
> Hard it was. I'd no time to pray
>
> This stone that here you Do see
> My Comerades erected for the sake of me.

Two smugglers, William Kemble and Andrew Gunton, were arraigned for the murder of this dragoon and an excise officer. The jury, much to the surprise of everyone, for the guilt of the prisoners

KITCHEN OF THE "GREEN MAN"

THE PEDDAR'S WAY

was undoubted, brought in a verdict of "Not guilty"; whereupon Mr. Murphy, counsel for the prosecution, moved for a new trial, observing that if a Norfolk jury were determined not to convict persons guilty of the most obvious crimes simply because, as smugglers, they commanded the sympathy of the country people, there was an end of all justice.

A second jury was forthwith empanelled and the evidence repeated, and after three hours' deliberation the prisoners were again found "Not guilty," and were, in accordance with that finding, acquitted and liberated.

It is abundantly possible that the foregoing incident had some connection with that locally favourite smugglers' route from the Norfolk coast inland, the Peddar's Way, which runs a long and lonely course from Holme, near Hunstanton, right through Norfolk into Suffolk, and is for the greater part of its length a broad, grassy track, romantically lined and overhung with fine trees. Such ancient ways, including the many old drove-roads in the north, never turnpiked, made capital soft going, and, rarely touching villages or hamlets, were of a highly desirable, secretive nature. The origin of the Peddar's, or Padder's, Way is still in dispute among antiquaries, some seeing in it a Roman road, others conceiving it to be a prehistoric track; but the broad, straight character of it seems to point to this long route having been Romanised. Its great age is evident on many accounts, not least among them being that the little town of Watton, near but not on it, is named from this prehistoric road, "Way-town," while that county division, the hundred, is the Hundred of Wayland.

CHAPTER X

THE DORSET AND DEVON COASTS—EPITAPHS AT KINSON AND WYKE—THE "WILTSHIRE MOON-RAKERS"—EPITAPH AT BRANSCOMBE—THE WARREN AND "MOUNT PLEASANT" INN

NOT so much smuggling incident as might be expected is found along the coasts of Dorset and Devon, but that is less on account of any lack of smuggling encounters in those parts than because less careful record has been kept of them. An early epitaph on a smuggler, to be seen in the churchyard of Kinson, just within the Dorset boundary, in an out-of-the-way situation at the back of Bournemouth, in a district formerly of almost trackless heaths, will sufficiently show that smuggling was active here:

> To the memory of Robert Trotman, late of Rowd, in the county of Wilts, who was barbarously murdered on the shore near Poole, the 24th March, 1765.
>
> A little tea, one leaf I did not steal,
> For guiltless bloodshed I to God appeal;
> Put tea in one scale, human blood in t'other
> And think what 'tis to slay a harmless brother.

This man was shot in an encounter with the revenue officers. He was one of a gang that used the church here as a hiding-place. The upper stage of the tower and an old altar-tomb were the favourite receptacles for their "free-trade" merchandise.

Trotman, it will be observed, was of Rowd, or

THE 'MOONRAKERS' 161

Rowde, in Wiltshire, two miles from Devizes, and was thus one of the "Wiltshire Moonrakers," whose descriptive title is due to smuggling history. Among the nicknames conferred upon the natives of our various shires and counties none is complimentary. They figure forth undesirable physical attributes, as when the Lincolnshire folk, dwellers among the fens, are styled "Yellow-bellies," *i. e.* frogs; or stupidity, *e. g.* "Silly Suffolk"; or humbug—for example, "Devonshire Crawlers." "Wiltshire Moonrakers" is generally considered to be a term of contempt for Wilts rustic stupidity; but, rightly considered, it is nothing of the kind. It all depends how you take the story which gave rise to it. The usual version tells us how a party of travellers, crossing a bridge in Wiltshire by night when the harvest moon was shining, observed a group of rustics raking in the stream, in which the great yellow disc of the moon was reflected. The travellers had the curiosity to ask them what it was they raked for in such a place and at so untimeous an hour; and were told they were trying to get "that cheese"—the moon—out of the water. The travellers went on their way amused with the simplicity of these "naturals," and spread the story far and wide.

But these apparently idiotic clodhoppers were wiser in their generation than commonly supposed, and were, in fact, smugglers surprised in the act of raking up a number of spirit-kegs that had been sunk in the bed of the stream until the arrival of a convenient season when they could with safety be removed. The travellers, properly considered, were really revenue officers, scouring the neighbourhood. This version of the story fairly throws the accusation of innocence and dunderheadedness back upon them, and clears the Wiltshire rural character from contempt. It should, however, be said that the first version of the story is generally told at the expense of the villagers of Bishop's Cannings, near Devizes, who have long writhed under a load of ancient satirical narratives, reflecting upon a lack of common sense alleged to be their chief characteristic.

Many of the western smuggling stories are of a humorous cast, rather than of the dreadful blood-boltered kind that disgraces the history of the home counties. Here is a case in point. On the evening of Sunday, July 10th, 1825, as two preventive men were on the look-out for smugglers, near Lulworth in Dorset, the smugglers, to the number of sixty or seventy, curiously enough, found them instead, and immediately taking away their swords and pistols, carried them to the edge of the cliff and placed them with their heads hanging over the precipice; with the comfortable assurance that if they made the least noise, or gave alarm, they should be immediately thrown over. In the interval a smuggling vessel landed a " crop " of one hundred casks, which the shore-gang placed on their horses and triumphantly carried away. The prisoners were then removed from their perilous position, and taken into an adjoining field, where they were bound hand and foot, and left overnight. They were found the next morning by their comrades, searching for them.

There are several points in this true tale that suggest it to have been the original whence Mr. Thomas Hardy obtained the chief motive of his short story, *The Distracted Preacher*.

IN DORSET

We do not find consecutive accounts of smuggling on this wild coast of Dorset; but when the veil is occasionally lifted and we obtain a passing glimpse, it is a picturesque scene that is disclosed. Thus, a furious encounter took place under St. Aldhelm's Head, in 1827, between an armed band of some seventy or eighty smugglers and the local preventive men, who numbered only ten, but gave a good account of themselves, two smugglers being reported killed on the spot, and many others wounded, while some of the preventive force, during the progress of the fight, quietly slipped to where the smugglers' boats had been left and made off with the goods stored in them.

"The smugglers are armed," says a report of this affair, "with swingels, like flails, with which they can knock people's brains out"; and proceeds to say that weapons of this kind, often delivering blows from unexpected quarters, are extremely difficult to fight against.

The captain of this gang was a man named Lucas, who kept an inn called the "Ship," at Woolbridge; and, information being laid, Captain Jackson, the local inspector of customs, went with an assistant and a police officer from London to his house at two o'clock in the morning and roused him.

"Who's there?" asked Lucas.

"Only I, Mrs. Smith's little girl. I want a drop of brandy for mother," returned the inspector, in a piping voice.

"Very well, my dear," said the landlord, and opened the door; to find himself in the grasp of the police-officer. Henry Fooks, of Knowle, and three others of the gang, were then arrested; and the whole five committed to Dorchester Gaol.

The wild coast of Dorset, if we except Poole Harbour and the cliffs of Purbeck, yields little to the inquirer in this sort, although there can be no doubt of smuggling having been in full operation here. Jack Rattenbury, whose story is told on another page, could doubtless have rubricated this shore of many cliffs and remote hamlets with striking instances; and not a cliff-top but must have frequently exhibited lights to "flash the lugger off," what time the preventive men were on the prowl; and no lonely strand but must have witnessed the smugglers, when the coast was again clear, rowing out and "creeping for the crop" that had been sunk and buoyed, or "put in the collar," as the saying went.

A relic of these for the most part unrecorded and forgotten incidents is found in the epitaph at Wyke, near Weymouth, on one William Lewis:

Sacred to the memory
of
WILLIAM LEWIS,
who was killed by a shot
from the *Pigmy* Schooner
21st April 1822, aged 53 years.

Of life bereft (by fell design),
I mingle with my fellow clay,
On God's protection I recline
To save me on the Judgment-day.

There shall each blood-stain'd soul appear,
Repent, all, ere it be too late,
Or Else a dreadful doom you'll hear,
For God will sure avenge my fate.

This Stone is Erected by his Wife
as the last mark of respect to an
Affectionate Husband.

The inscription is surmounted by a representation, carved in low relief, of the *Pigmy* schooner chasing the smuggling vessel.

Old folk, now gone from the scene of their reminiscences, used to tell of this tragedy, and of the landing of the body of the unfortunate Lewis on the rocks of Sandsfoot Castle, where the ragged, roofless walls of that old seaward fortress impend over the waves, and the great bulk of Portland isle glooms in mid distance upon the bay. They tell, too, how the inscription was long kept gilded by his relatives; but the last trace of it has long since vanished.

Many miles intervene, and another county must be entered, before another tragical epitaph bearing upon smuggling is found. If you go to Seaton, in South Devon, and walk inland from the modern developments of that now rapidly growing town to the old church, you may see there a tablet recording the sad fate of William Henry Paulson, midshipman of H.M.S. *Queen Charlotte*, and eight seamen, who all perished in a gale of wind off Sidmouth, while cruising in a galley after smugglers, in the year 1816.

A few miles westward, through Beer to Branscombe, the country is of a very wild and lonely kind. In the weird, eerie churchyard of Branscombe, in which astonishing epitaphs of all kinds abound, is a variant upon the smugglers' violent ends, in the inscription to one " Mr. John Harley, Custom House Officer of this parish." It proceeds to narrate how, " as he was endeavouring to extinguish some Fire made between Beer and Seaton as a signal to a Smuggling Boat then off at sea, he fell by some means or other from the top of the cliff to the bottom, by which he was unfortunately killed. This unhappy accident happened the 9th day of

August in the year of our Lord 1755, *ætatis suæ* 45. He was an active and diligent officer and very inoffensive in his life and conversation."

So here was another martyr to the conditions created by bad government.

The estuary of the Exe, between Exmouth and Starcross, was for many years greatly favoured by smugglers, for, as may readily be perceived to this day, there lay in the two-miles-broad channel, where sea and river mingle, a wide, wild stretch of sand, almost awash at high water, heaped up in towans overgrown with tussocks of coarse, sour grasses, or sinking into hollows full of brackish water: pleasant in daytime, but a dangerous place at night. Here, in this islanded waste, there were no roads nor tracks at all, and few were those who ever came to disturb the curlews or the seabirds that nested, unafraid. In these twentieth-century times of ours the Warren—for such is the name of this curiously amphibious place—has become a place of picnic parties on summer afternoons, largely by favour of the Great Western Railway having provided, midway between the stations of Starcross and Dawlish, a little platform called the "Warren Halt." But in those times before railways, when the Warren was not easily come at, the smugglers found it a highly convenient place for their business. Beside it, under the lee of Langston Point, there is a sheltered strand, and, at such times when it was considered quite safe, the sturdy free-traders quietly ran their boats ashore here, on the yellow sands, and conveyed their contents to the "Mount Pleasant" inn, which is an unassuming—and was in those times a still more unassuming—house, perched picturesquely on the crest of a red sand-

THE WARREN

stone bluff which rises inland, sheer from the marshy meadows. It was a very convenient receiving-house and signal-station for all of this trade, for it owned caverns hollowed out of the red sandstone in places inaccessible to the authorities, and from its isolated height, overlooking the flats, could easily communicate encouragement or warning to friends anxiously riding at anchor out at sea. The lights that flashed on dark and tempestuous nights from its high-hung rustic balcony were significant. The only man who could have told much of the smugglers' secrets here was the unfortunate Lieutenant Palk, who lay wait one such night upon the Warren. But dead men tell no tales; and that ill-starred officer was found in the morning, drowned, face downwards, in a shallow pool, whether by accident or design there was nothing to show. As already remarked, the Warren was a dangerous place to wander in after dark.

It is quite vain nowadays to seek for the smugglers' caves at Mount Pleasant. They were long ago filled up.

In these times the holiday-maker, searching for shells, is the only feature of the sands that fringe the seaward edge of the Warren. It is a fruitful hunting-ground for such, especially after rough weather. But the day following a storm was, in those times, the opportunity of the local revenue men, who, forming a strong party, were used to take boat and pull down here and thoroughly search the foreshore; for at such times any spirit-tubs that might have been sunk out at sea and carefully buoyed by the smugglers, awaiting a favourable time for landing, were apt to break loose and drift in-shore. There was always, at such times, a sporting chance of a good haul. But, on the other hand, some of the many tubs that had been sunk months before, and lost, would on these occasions come to hand, and they were worth just nothing at all: long immersion in salt water having spoiled their contents, with the result that what had been right good hollands or cognac had become a peculiarly ill-savoured liquid, which smelt to heaven when it was broached. The revenue people called this abominable stuff, which, as Shakespeare might say, had " suffered a sea-change into something new and strange," by the appropriate name of " stinkibus."

CHAPTER XI

CORNWALL IN SMUGGLING STORY—CRUEL COPPINGER—HAWKER'S SKETCH—THE FOWEY SMUGGLERS—TOM POTTER, OF POLPERRO—THE DEVILS OF TALLAND—SMUGGLERS' EPITAPHS—CAVE AT WENDRON—ST IVES

CORNWALL is the region of romance: the last corner of England in which legend and imagination had full play, while matter-of-fact already sat enthroned over the rest of the land. At a time when newspapers almost everywhere had already long been busily recording facts, legends were still in the making throughout this westernmost part of the island. We may, in our innocence, style Cornwall a part of England; but the Cornish do not think of it as such, and when they cross the Tamar into Devonshire will still often speak of "going into England." They are historically correct in doing so, for this is the unconquered land of the Cornu-Welsh, never assimilated by the Saxon kingdoms. Historically and ethnologically, the Cornish are a people apart.

The Coppinger legend is a case in point, illustrating the growth of wild stories out of meagre facts. " Cruel Coppinger " is a half-satanic, semi-Viking character in the tales of North Cornwall and North Devon, of whom no visitor is likely to remain ignorant for not only was he a dread figure of local folklore from about the first quarter of the nineteenth century, but he was written up in 1866 by the Reverend R. S. Hawker, Vicar of Morwenstow, who not only collated those floating stories, but added very much of his own, for Hawker was a man—and a not very scrupulous man—of imagination. Hawker's presentment of "Cruel Coppinger" was published in a popular magazine, and then the legend became full-blown.

The advent of Coppinger upon the coast at Welcombe Mouth, near where Devon and Cornwall join, was dramatic. The story tells how a strange vessel went to pieces on the reefs and how only one person escaped with his life, in the midst of a howling tempest. This was the skipper, a Dane named Coppinger. On the beach, on foot and on horseback, was a crowd, waiting, in the usual Cornish way, for any wreck of the sea that might be thrown up. Into the midst of them, like some sea-monster, dashed this sole survivor, and bounded suddenly upon the crupper of a young damsel who had ridden to the shore to see the sight. He grasped her bridle, and, shouting in a foreign tongue, urged the doubly-laden animal to full speed, and the horse naturally took his usual way home. The damsel was Miss Dinah Hamlyn. The stranger descended at her father's door and lifted her off her saddle. He then announced himself as a Dane, named Coppinger, and took his place at the family board and there remained until he had secured the affections and hand of Dinah. The father died, and Coppinger succeeded to the management and control of the house, which thenceforward became the refuge of every lawless character along the coast. All kinds of wild uproar and reckless revelry appalled the neighbourhood, night and day. It was discovered that an organised band of smugglers, wreckers, and poachers made this house their rendezvous, and that "Cruel Coppinger" was their captain. In those times no revenue officer durst exercise vigilance west of the Tamar, and, to put an end at once to all such surveillance, the head of a gauger was chopped off by one of Coppinger's gang, on the gunwale of a boat.

Strange vessels began to appear at regular intervals on the coast, and signals were flashed from the headlands, to lead them into the safest creek or cove. Amongst these, one, a full-rigged schooner, soon became ominously conspicuous. She was for long the terror of those shores, and her name was the *Black Prince*. Once, with Coppinger aboard, she led a revenue cutter into an intricate channel near the Bull Rock, where, from knowledge of the bearings, the *Black Prince* escaped scathless, while the King's vessel perished with all on board. In those times, if any landsman became obnoxious to Coppinger's men he was seized and carried aboard the *Black Prince*, and obliged to save his life by enrolling himself as one of the crew.

Amid such practices, ill-gotten gold began to accrue to Coppinger. At one time he had enough money to purchase a freehold farm bordering on the sea. When the day of transfer came, he and one of his followers appeared before the lawyer and paid the money in dollars, ducats, doubloons, and pistoles. The lawyer objected, but Coppinger, with an oath, bade him take that or none.

Long impunity increased Coppinger's daring. Over certain bridle-paths along the fields he exercised exclusive control, and issued orders that no man was to pass over them by night. They were known as "Coppinger's Tracks," and all converged at a cliff called "Steeple Brink." Here the precipice fell sheer to the sea, 300 feet, with overhanging eaves a hundred feet from the summit. Under this part was a cave, to be reached only by a rope-ladder from above. This was "Coppinger's Cave." Here sheep were tethered to the rock and fed on stolen hay and corn until slaughtered. Kegs of brandy and hollands were piled around; chests of tea, and iron-bound sea-chests contained the chattels and revenues of the Coppinger royalty of the sea.

The terror linked with Coppinger's name throughout the north coasts of Cornwall and Devon was so extreme that the people themselves, wild and lawless though they were, submitted to his sway as though he had been lord of the soil and they his vassals. Such a household as his was, of course, far from happy or calm. Although, when his father-in-law died, he had insensibly acquired possession of the stock and farm, there remained in the hands of the widow a considerable amount of money. This he obtained from the helpless woman by instalments and by force. He would fasten his wife to the pillar of her oak bedstead, and call her mother into the room, and assure her he would flog Dinah with a cat-o'-nine-tails till her mother had transferred to him what he wanted. This act of brutal cruelty he repeated until he had utterly exhausted the widow's store.

There was but one child of Coppinger's marriage. It was a boy, and deaf and dumb, but mischievous and ungovernable, delighting in cruelty to other children, animals, or birds. When he was but six years of age, he was found one day, hugging himself with delight, and pointing down from the brink of a cliff to the beach, where the body of a neighbour's child was found; and it was believed that little Coppinger had flung him over. It was a saying in the district that, as a judgment on his father's cruelty, the child had been born without a human soul.

But the end arrived. Money became scarce, and more than one armed King's cutter was seen, day and night, hovering off the land. And at last Coppinger, "who came with the water, went with the wind." A wrecker, watching the shore, saw, as the sun went down, a full-rigged vessel standing off and on. Coppinger came to the beach, put off in a boat to the vessel, and jumped aboard. She spread canvas, and was seen no more. That night was one of storm, and whether the vessel rode it out or not, none ever knew.

It is hardly necessary to add that the Coppinger of these and other rumbustious stories is a strictly unhistorical Coppinger; and that, in short, they are mainly efforts of Hawker's own imagination, built upon very slight folklore traditions.

Who and what, however, was the real Coppinger? Very little exact information is available, but what we have entirely demolishes the legendary halfman, half-monster of those remarkable exploits.

Daniel Herbert Copinger, or Coppinger, was wrecked at Welcombe Mouth on December 23rd, 1792, and was given shelter beneath the roof of Mr. William Arthur, yeoman farmer, at Golden Park, Hartland, where for many years afterwards his name might have been seen, scratched on a windowpane :

D. H. Coppinger, shipwrecked December 23 1792, kindly received by Mr. Wm. Arthur.

There is not the slightest authority for the story of his sensational leap on to the saddle of Miss Dinah Hamlyn; but it is true enough that the next year he married a Miss Hamlyn—her Christian name was Ann—elder of the two daughters of Ackland Hamlyn, of Galsham, in Hartland, and in the registers of Hartland church may be found this entry: " Daniel Herbert Coppinger, of the King's Royal Navy, and Ann Hamlyn mard. (by licence) 3 Aug." The " damsel " of the story also turns out, by the cold, calm evidence of this entry, to have been of the mature age of forty-two.

Mrs. Hamlyn, Coppinger's mother-in-law, died in 1800, and was buried in the chancel of Hartland church. It is, of course, quite possible that his married life was stormy and that he, more or less by force, extracted money from Mrs. Hamlyn, and he was certainly more or less involved in smuggling. But that he, or any of his associates, chopped off the head of an excise officer is not to be credited. Tales are told of revenue officers searching at Galsham for contraband, and of Mrs. Coppinger hurriedly hiding a quantity of valuable silks in the kitchen oven, while her husband engaged their attention in permitting them to find a number of spirit-kegs, which they presently found, much to their disgust, to be empty; and, moreover, empty so long that scarce the ghost of even a smell of the departed spirit could be traced. But the flurried Mrs. Coppinger had in her haste done a disastrous thing, for the oven was in baking trim, and the valuable silks were baked to a cinder.

Little else is known of Coppinger, and nothing whatever of his alleged connection with the Navy. He became bankrupt in 1802, and was then a prisoner in the King's Bench Prison. With him was one Richard Copinger, said to have been a merchant in Martinique. Nothing is known of him after this date, but rumour told how he was living apart from his wife, at Barnstaple, and subsisting on an allowance from her.

Mrs. Coppinger herself, in after years, resided at Barnstaple, and died there on August 31st, 1833. She lies buried in the chancel of Hartland church beside her mother.

According to the Rev. S. Baring-Gould, Coppinger was not really a Dane, but an Irishman, and had a wife at Trewhiddle near St. Austell. He, on the same authority, is said to have done extremely well as a smuggler, and had not only a farm at Trewhiddle, but another at Roscoff, in Brittany. A daughter, says Mr. Baring-Gould, married a Trefusis, son of Lord Clinton, and Coppinger gave her £40,000 as a dowry. A son married the daughter of Sir John Murray, Bart., of Stanhope. The source of this interesting information is not stated. It appears wildly improbable.

Hawker very cleverly embodied the smuggling sentiment of Cornwall in a sketch he wrote, styled " The Light of Other Days."

" It was full six in the evening of an autumn day when a traveller arrived where the road ran along by a sandy beach just above high-water mark. The stranger, who was a native of some inland town, and utterly unacquainted with Cornwall and its ways, had reached the brink of the tide just as a ' landing ' was coming off. It was a scene not only to instruct a townsman, but to dazzle and surprise. At sea, just beyond the billows, lay the vessel, well moored with anchors at stem and stern.

Between the ship and the shore, boats, laden to the gunwale, passed to and fro. Crowds assembled on the beach to help the cargo ashore. On one hand a boisterous group surrounded a keg with the head knocked in, for simplicity of access to the good cognac, into which they dipped whatsoever vessel came first to hand; one man had filled his shoe. On the other side they fought and wrestled, cursed and swore. Horrified at what he saw, the stranger lost all self-command, and, oblivious of personal danger, he began to shout, ' What a horrible sight! Have you no shame? Is there no magistrate at hand? Cannot any justice of the peace be found in this fearful country?'

" ' No; thanks be to God,' answered a gruff, hoarse voice. ' None within eight miles.'

" ' Well, then,' screamed the stranger, ' is there no clergyman hereabout? Does no minister of the parish live among you on this coast?'

" ' Aye, to be sure there is,' said the same deep voice.

" ' Well, how far off does he live? Where is he?'

" ' That's he, yonder, sir, with the lantern.'

" And, sure enough, there he stood on a rock, and poured, with pastoral diligence, ' the light of other days ' on a busy congregation."

The complete, true story of smuggling along the Cornish Coast will never be told. Those who could have contributed illuminating chapters to it, and would not, are dead, and those who now would are reduced to seeking details and finding only scraps. But some of these scraps are not unpalatable.

Thus we have the story of that Vicar of Maker whose church was used as a smugglers' store. The

"THE LIGHT OF OTHER DAYS"

vicar was not a party to these proceedings, as may well be judged by his inviting his rural dean to ascend to the roof of the church-tower with him, for sake of the view : the view disclosing not only a lovely expanse of sea and wooded foreshore, but also a heap of twenty-three spirit-kegs, reposing in the gutters between the roofs of nave and aisle.

The " Fowey Gallants," as the townsfolk of that little seaport delighted to call themselves—the title having descended from Elizabethan and even earlier times, when the " Gallants " in question were, in plain speech, nothing less than turbulent seafaring rowdies and pirates—were not behind other Cornish folk in their smuggling enterprises. That prime authority on this part of the Cornish coast, Jonathan Couch, historian of Polperro, tells us of an exciting incident at Fowey, in the smuggling way. On one occasion, the custom-house officers heard of an important run that had taken place overnight, and accordingly sent out scouts in every direction to locate the stuff, if possible. At Landaviddy one of these parties met a farm-labourer whom they suspected of having taken part in the run. They taxed him with it, and tried him all ways; without effect, until they threatened to impress him for service in the Navy unless he revealed the hiding-place of the cognac. His resolution broke down at that, and he told how the kegs had been hidden in a large cave at Yellow Rock, which the officers then instructed him to mark with a chalk cross.

The revenue men then went off for reinforcements, and, returning, met an armed band of smugglers, who had taken up a strong position at New Quay Head. They were armed with sticks, cutlasses, and muskets, and had brought a loaded gun upon the scene, which they trained upon the cave; while a man with flaring portfire stood by and dared the officers to remove the goods. Official prudence counselled the revenue men to retire for further support; but when they had again returned the smugglers had disappeared, and the kegs with them.

Fowey's trade in "moonshine," *i. e.* contraband spirits, was, like that of the Cornish coast in general, with Roscoff, in Brittany; and a regular service was maintained for years. As late as 1832 the luggers *Eagle*, thirty-five tons; *Rose*, eleven tons; and *Dove*, of the same burthen, were well known in the trade. Among the smuggling craft belonging to Polperro, the *Unity* was said to have made upwards of five hundred entirely successful trips.

The Polperro men went far and worked overtime at smuggling. Dr. Jonathan Couch, who resided there, tells the picturesque story of the *Lottery* and Tom Potter, of Polperro, but he tells it so insufficiently and with such inaccuracy that the real, authentic history demands to be set forth.

The key to this dramatic incident in the history of smuggling is found in the *Naval Chronicle* of 1798, which under date of December 27th has the following item of news:—"Last night, about ten o'clock, Humphrey Glynn, an officer of the Customs, belonging to a boat stationed at Cawsand, whilst in the execution of his duty, was shot by a party of smugglers and died instantly. The boat in which he was killed was commanded by Mr. Ambrose Bowden, who, together with the deceased and three other officers, fell in with a very large smuggling cutter about three miles south of Penlee Point, lying at anchor and just going to put her cargo into boats, then alongside her, for the purpose of landing at Cawsand. When Mr. Bowden got within hail of the smugglers he gave them to understand what his boat was, upon which they immediately fired point-blank into her, and repeated the fire many times, the second or third of which struck the deceased and carried away the whole front of his head, when he dropped and expired immediately. The fire was returned from the boat, and kept up so gallantly that the smuggler cut her cable and put to sea without effecting the landing of the cargo."

So far, at any rate, the fortunes of the day, or rather of the night, were with the smugglers. The *Lottery* then disappeared from the scene; and we hear of her next only through another item of news in the *Naval Chronicle*, May 18th, 1799, " Arrived at Plymouth the *Hinde*, revenue cutter, with the *Lottery* smuggler, having on board 400 ankers of Spirits; she threw overboard 200 ankers in the chase."

The subsequent trial of the crew of the *Lottery* supplies details wherewith to embellish that bald account. It appeared that the revenue cutter *Hinde*, commanded by Captain Gabriel Bray, was cruising off the Start, and at about 3 p.m. on May 13th, 1799, observed a large cutter, presently identified as the *Lottery*, making for the shore. So soon as the smuggler observed the *Hinde*, she altered her course and put about for Bolt Head to the westward. Chase was continued throughout the night. By five o'clock next morning the two vessels were off the Lizard, five miles apart, when their further progress was stopped by a calm; whereupon Captain Bray sent two of his boats, duly armed, and under command of the mate, Hugh Pearce, to take possession of the smuggler, the revenue flag being at the same time hoisted on the *Hinde,* and a gun fired. As the boats drew near the smuggler, whose crew were desperately endeavouring to row the vessel away with long sweeps, a gun was fired at them, and a man calling through a speaking-trumpet to " Keep off them boats, immediately ! " The mate of the *Hinde* then rowed up to within a cable's length of the smuggler, when he was again warned that if the boats did not keep off they would be fired upon and sunk. He stood up and shouted to them that they were the *Hinde's* boats, and that he had orders to board the vessel; orders he must obey. He further added, that he knew the vessel. It was the *Lottery,* and that he knew the men aboard. Someone aboard rejoined that they cared not a damn who the boat belonged to, or who happened to be in it; that the vessel was not the *Lottery ;* and that unless the boats kept off they would be fired upon, and all in them killed. The mate observed that the vessel's name on the stern had been covered over with canvas. He also observed that during these parleyings three guns had been run out, and that a man with a musket stood ready to fire. Bearing in mind the fate that had overtaken Glynn, five months earlier, in dealing with these same desperate men, he thought it prudent to withdraw.

The boats had not long returned to the *Hinde* when a breeze sprang up. Both vessels made sail, but the revenue cutter, proving the better, and gaining on the *Lottery,* the smugglers thereupon threw much of their contraband overboard. Still the *Hinde* gained, and at two o'clock in the afternoon, off the Longships, her chase-guns were brought to bear. Observing this, the smugglers shortened sail, lowered their boat, and twelve of them jumping in, rowed as fast as they could for shore. The two boats of the *Hinde* were then sent in pursuit, and captured them half-way. At the same time the *Lottery* herself was taken, with five men aboard, and a cargo comprising 716 casks of gin, with some tea and tobacco. The *Lottery*, instead of, as was often the case, being condemned and destroyed, was taken into the revenue service, and performed some smart work on her new commissions. Thus we read, " October 25th, 1799. Plymouth : came in, the *Lottery*, revenue vessel, with the *Assistance*, smuggler, from Guernsey, with a cargo which the *Lottery* gallantly cut out of Polperro Bay."

The majority of the smugglers of the *Lottery* captured off the Longships had meanwhile been tried and sentenced, but there remained the more serious affair of the killing of Humphrey Glynn in the previous December to be disposed of. Roger Toms, implicated to some degree in it, was among the captured smugglers, and, " to save his life," as he expressed himself, gave an account of the affair, implicating among his comrades William Searle, Thomas Ventin and Thomas Potter. On the charge of wilful murder they were brought up at the Old Bailey, December 20th, 1799, but the principal witness, Roger Toms, King's Evidence, could not be found. He had been mysteriously spirited away, as the prosecution stated, from the custody in which for his own safety, he had been kept, aboard a revenue cutter at Fowey. Application was therefore made, and granted, to postpone the trial until he could be found. He had been, as a matter of fact, lured ashore and hidden in a cave on the coast of Cornwall by his neighbours and associates still at large, and was eventually conveyed to Guernsey, and was there on the point of being smuggled over to America, when he succeeded in making himself known to the revenue officers, and so was rescued and brought up as a Crown witness at the trial, finally held at the Old Bailey, December 10th, 1800.

The evidence is interesting. It appeared that the night of that two-year-old tragedy was one of brilliant moonshine, and that all the unloading operations of the *Lottery* could be distinctly observed. When the revenue boat was seen approaching, the smugglers hailed the men to keep off, or they would be fired upon. Bowden replied that he was a revenue officer, and they might fire if they pleased. He then stood up and unfurled the revenue flag, whereupon the smugglers made good their promise, and opened fire. When three shots had been discharged, Bowden saw the oar fall from the hand of the second man, and called to him, not thinking he had been hit, to "mind what he was about." The bowman then exclaimed "Glynn is shot!" Bowman, taking up a musket, returned the smugglers' fire, which was briskly replied to. The *Lottery* then cut her cable, and escaped. Glynn was found to be quite dead, the fore part of his skull having been blown away.

Toms deposed that he was a mariner aboard the *Lottery* cutter on the night in question. Their cargo consisted of spirits, and they had just dispatched several boatloads to Cawsand, when he went below.

While between-decks he heard voices cry " Keep off," and " It's a King's boat." There was then firing, and presently orders were given to cut the cable, and they then ran before the wind to Polperro. A conversation then took place between Oliver, the master, and Potter, Searle, and another, the former saying " He should be sorry if any harm had taken place by their firing ; " and Potter replying that " He had taken good level when he fired, and was sure that he saw a man drop." Toms said, further, that at the time the firing took place, Ventin, the cook, was sent below into the cabin by Oliver, to make the pokers red-hot, with a view to firing the swivel guns, if necessary ; and that after the cable had been cut he went on deck and heard Searle say that " he was glad the boat had been kept off ; that he had fired, but meant to do no harm, and hoped he had done none."

Searle and Ventin were acquitted, but Potter was convicted, and was hanged on December 18th at Execution Dock, Wapping.

Talland, midway between Polperro and Looe, was a favourite spot with these daring Polperro fellows. It offered better opportunities than those given by Polperro itself for unobserved landings ; for it was—and it still is—a weird, lonely place, overhanging the sea, with a solitary ancient church well within sound of the waves that beat heavily upon the little sands. It was an easy matter to store kegs in the churchyard itself, and to take them inland, or into Polperro by the country roads, when opportunity offered, hidden in carts taking seaweed for manure to the fields.

At one time Talland owned a shuddery reputation

in all this country-side, and people in the farmhouses told, with many a fearful glance over their shoulders, of the uncanny creatures that nightly haunted the churchyard. Devils, wraiths, and fearful apparitions made the spot a kind of satanic parliament; and we may be amply sure that these horrid stories lost no accent or detail of terror by constant repetition in those ingle-nooks on winter evenings. This is not to say that other places round about were innocent of things supernatural; for those were times when every Cornish glen, moor, stream, and hill had their bukkadhus, their piskies, and gnomes of sorts, good and evil; but the infernal company that consorted together in Talland churchyard was entirely beside these old-established creatures. They were *hors concours*, as the French would say : they formed a class by themselves; and, in the expressive slang of to-day, they were " the Limit," the *ne plus ultra* of militant ghostdom. People rash enough to take the church-path through Talland after night had fallen were sure to hear and see strange, semi-luminous figures; and they bethought them then of the at once evil and beneficent reputation owned and really enjoyed by Parson Dodge, the eccentric clergyman of Talland, who was reputed an exorcist of the first quality. He it was who, doughty wrestler with the most obstinate spectres, found himself greatly in demand in a wide geographical area for the banishing of troublesome ghosts for a long term of years to the Red Sea; but it was whispered, on the other hand, that he kept a numerous band of diabolic familiars believed by the simple folk of that age to resort nightly to the vicarage for their orders, and then to do his bidding. These were the spiteful

THE DEVILS OF TALLAND

THE DEVILS OF TALLAND

creatures, thought the country people, who, to revenge themselves for this servitude, lurked in the churchyard, and got even with mankind by pinching and smacking and playing all manner of scurvy tricks upon those who dared pass this way under cover of night. Uncle Zack Chowne even got a black eye by favour of these inimical agencies, one exceptionally dark night when, coming home along this way, under the influence of spirits not of supernatural origin, he met a posse of fiends, and, in the amiable manner of the completely intoxicated, insisted upon their adjourning with him to the nearest inn, "jush for shake of ole timesh." In fact, he made the sad mistake of taking the fiends in question for friends, and addressed them by name: with the result that he got a sledge-hammer blow in what the prize-fighting brotherhood used to call "the peeper."

If he had adopted the proper method to be observed when meeting spirits, *i. e.* if he had stood up and "said his Nummy Dummy," all would doubtless have been well; this form of exorcism being in Cornwall of great repute and never known to fail: being nothing less, indeed, than the Latin *In Nomine Domine* in disguise.

But the real truth of the matter, as the readers of these lines who can see further through a brick wall than others may readily perceive, was that those savage spooks and mischievous, Puck-like shapes were really youthful local smugglers in disguise, engaged at one and the same time in a highly profitable nocturnal business, and in taking the welcome opportunity thus offered in an otherwise dull circle of establishing a glorious "rag."

Parson Dodge himself was something more than suspected of being "ower sib" to these at once commercial and rollicking dogs, and Talland was in fact the scene of many a successful run that could scarce have been successful had not this easy-going cleric amiably permitted.

It is thus peculiarly appropriate that we find to-day in this lonely churchyard an epitaph upon one Robert Mark. It is a tragical enough epitaph, its tragedy perhaps disguised at the first glance by the grotesquely comic little cherubs carved upon the tombstone, and representing the local high-water mark of mortuary sculpture a hundred years or so ago. They are pursy cherubs, of oleaginous appearance and of this-worldly, rather than of other-worldly paunch and deportment. In general, Talland churchyard is rich in such carvings; death's-heads of appalling ugliness to be seen in company with middle-aged, double-chinned angels wearing what look suspiciously like chest-protectors and pyjamas, and they decorate, with weirdly humorous aspect, the monuments and ledger stones, and grin familiarly from the pavement with the half-obliterated grins of many generations back. One of them points with a claw, intended for a hand, to an object somewhat resembling a crumpled dress-tie set up on end, probably designed to represent an hour-glass.

Such is the mortuary art of these lonesome parishes in far Cornwall: naïve, uninstructed, home-made. It sufficed the simple folk for whom it was wrought; and now that more conventional and pretentious memorials have taken its place, to serve the turn of folk less simple, there are those who would abolish its uncouth manifestations. But that way—with

'Oft, from yon solemn and bat-haunted tow'r
The smugglers issue at the midnight hour.'

Butler

the urbanities of the world—goes old Cornwall, never to be replaced.

Here is the epitaph to

ROBERT MARK;
late of Polperro, who Unfortunately was ſhot at Sea the 24th day of Jany. in the year of our Lord GOD 1802, in the 40th Year of His AGE

In prime of Life moſt suddenly,
  Sad tidings to relate;
Here view My utter destiny,
  And pity, My sad state:
I by a ſhot, which Rapid flew,
  Was inſtantly ſtruck dead;
LORD pardon the Offender who
  My precious blood did ſhed.
Grant Him to reſt, and forgive Me,
  All I have done amiſs;
And that I may Rewarded be
  With Everlasting Bliſs.

Robert Mark was at the helm of a boat which had been obliged to run before a revenue cutter. It was at the point of escaping when the cutter's crew opened fire upon the fugitive, killing the helmsman on the spot. He had been one of the crew of the *Lottery* in the affair of 1799, and had served a term of imprisonment in connection with it; and had not long been at liberty when thus he met his end.

Let us trust he has duly won to that everlasting bliss that not even smugglers are denied. The mild and forgiving terms of the epitaph are to be noted with astonishment; the usual run of sentiment to be observed on the very considerable number of these memorials to smugglers cut off suddenly in the plenitude of their youth and beauty being particularly revengeful and bloodthirsty, or, at the best, bitterly reproachful.

Among these many epitaphs on smugglers to be met with in the churchyards of seaboard parishes is the following, to be found in the water-side parish of Mylor, near Falmouth. Details of the incident in which this " Cus-toms house officer ") spelled here exactly as the old lettering on the tombstone has it) shot and mortally wounded Thomas James appear to have been altogether lost :

> We have not a moment we can call our own.
>
> In Memory of Thomas James, aged 35 years, who on the evening of the 7th Dec. 1814, on his returning to Flushing from St. Mawes in a boat was shot by a Cus-toms house officer and expired a few days after.
>
> Officious zeal in luckless hour laid wait
> And wilful sent the murderous ball of fate :
> James to his home, which late in health he left,
> Wounded returned—of life is soon bereft.

This is quite a mild and academic example, and obviously the work of some passionless hireling, paid for his verses. He would have written not less affectingly for poor dog Tray.

Prussia Cove, the most famous smuggling centre in Cornwall, finds mention in another chapter. Little else remains to be said, authentically at any rate. Invention, however, could readily people every cove with desperate men and hair-raising encounters, and there could nowadays be none who should be able to deny the truth of them. But we will leave all that to the novelists, merely pointing out that facts continually prove themselves at least as strange as fiction. Thus at Wendron, five miles inland from Helston, two caves, or underground chambers, were discovered in 1905 during some alterations and rebuildings, close to the churchyard. Local opinion declared them to be smugglers' hiding-holes.

KNILL OF ST. IVES

There stands in St. Ives town a ruined old mansion in one of the narrow alley-ways. It is known as Hicks' Court, and must have been a considerable place, in its day. Also the owners of it must have been uncommonly fond of good liquors, for it has a "secret" cellar, so called no doubt because, like the "secret" drawers of bureaus, its existence was perfectly obvious. Locally it is known as a "smugglers' store."

In such a place as St. Ives, on a coast of old so notorious for smuggling, we naturally look for much history in this sort, but research fails to reward even the most diligent; and we have to be content with the meagre suspicions (for they were nothing more) of the honesty of John Knill, a famous native and resident of the town in the second half of the eighteenth century, who was Collector of Customs in that port, and in 1767 was chosen Mayor. His action in equipping some small craft to serve as privateers against smugglers was wilfully misconstrued; and, at any rate, it does not seem at all fitting that he, as an official of the customs service, should have been concerned in such private ventures. These "privateers," it was said locally, were themselves actively employed in smuggling.

He was also, according to rumour, responsible, together with one Praed, of Trevetho, for a ship which was driven ashore in St. Ives Bay, and, when boarded by Roger Wearne, customs officer, was found to be deserted by captain and crew, who had been careful to remove all the ship's papers, so that her owners remained unknown. The vessel was found to be full of contraband goods, including a great quantity of china, some of it of excellent quality. Wearne conceived the brilliant idea of taking some samples of the best for his own personal use, and filled out the baggy breeches he was wearing with them, before he made to rejoin the boat that had put him aboard. This uncovenanted cargo made his movements, as he came over the side, so slow that one of his impatient boatmen smartly whacked him with the flat of his oar, calling, " Look sharp, Wearne," and was dismayed when, in place of the thud that might have been expected, there came a crash like the falling of a trayful of crockery, followed by a cry of dismay and anguish.

CHAPTER XII

TESTIMONY TO THE QUALITIES OF THE SEAFARING SMUGGLERS—ADAM SMITH ON SMUGGLING—A CLERICAL COUNTERBLAST—BIOGRAPHICAL SKETCHES OF SMUGGLERS—ROBERT JOHNSON, HARRY PAULET—WILLIAM GIBSON, A CONVERTED SMUGGLER

CARE has already been taken to discriminate between the hardy, hearty, and daring fellows who brought their duty-free goods across the sea and those others who, daring also, but often cruel and criminal, handled the goods ashore. We now come to close quarters with the seafaring smugglers, in a few biographical sketches: premising them with some striking testimony to their qualities as seamen.

Captain Brenton, in his *History of the Royal Navy*, pays a very high, but not extravagant, compliment to these daring fellows: "These men," he says, "are as remarkable for their skill in seamanship as for their audacity in the hour of danger; their local knowledge has been highly advantageous to the Navy, into which, however, they never enter, unless sent on board ships of war as a punishment for some crime committed against the revenue laws. They are hardy, sober, and faithful to each other, beyond the generality of seamen; and, when shipwreck occurs, have been known to perform deeds not exceeded in any country in the world; probably unequalled in the annals of other maritime powers."

Such men as these, besides being, in the rustic opinion, very much of heroes, engaged in an unequal warfare, against heavy odds, with a hateful, ogreish abstraction called " the Government," which existed only for the purpose of taxing and suppressing the poor, for the benefit of the rich, were regarded as benefactors; for they supplied the downtrodden, overtaxed people with better articles, at lower prices, than could be obtained in the legitimate way of traders who had paid excise duties.

There was probably a considerable basis of truth to support this view, for there is no doubt that duty-paid goods were largely adulterated. To adulterate his spirits, his tea, and his tobacco was the nearest road to any considerable profit that the tradesman could then make.

Things being of this complexion, it would have been the sheerest pedantry to refuse to purchase the goods the free-traders supplied at such alluringly low prices, and of such indubitably excellent quality; and to give retail publicans and shopkeepers and private consumers their due, as sensible folk, untroubled by super-sensitive consciences, they rarely did refuse.

Adam Smith, in the course of his writings on political economy, nearly a century and a half ago, stated the popular view about smuggling and the purchase of smuggled goods :

" To pretend to have any scruple about buying smuggled goods, though a manifest encouragement to the violation of the revenue laws, and to the perjury which almost always attends it, would in most countries be regarded as one of those pedantic pieces of hypocrisy which, instead of gaining credit with anybody, seems only to expose the person who

THE PARSONS

affects to practise it to the suspicion of being a greater knave than most of his neighbours."

From even the most charitable point of view, that person who was so eccentric as to refuse to take advantage of any favourable opportunity of purchasing cheaply such good stuff as might be offered to him, and had not paid toll to the revenue, was a prig.

Smith himself looked upon the smuggler with a great deal of sympathy, and regarded him as " a person who, though no doubt blamable for violating the laws of his country, is frequently incapable of violating those of natural justice, and would have been in every respect an excellent citizen had not the laws of his country made that a crime which nature never meant to be so."

Very few, indeed, were those voices raised against the practice of smuggling. Among them, however, was that of John Wesley, perhaps the most influential of all, especially in the west of England. The clergy in general might rail against the smugglers, but there were few among them who did not enjoy the right sort of spirits which, singularly enough, could only commonly be obtained from these shy sources; and there was a certain malignant satisfaction to any properly constituted smuggler in using the tower, or perhaps even the pulpit, of a parish church as temporary spirit-cellar, and in undermining the parson's honesty by the present of a tub. Few were those reverend persons who repudiated this sly suggestion of co-partnery, and those few who felt inclined so to do were generally silenced by the worldly wisdom of their parish clerks, who, forming as it were a connecting link between things sacred and profane, could on occasion inform a clergyman that his most respected churchwarden was financially interested in the success of some famous run of goods just notoriously brought off.

Among those few clergy who actively disapproved of these things we must include the Rev. Robert Hardy, somewhat multitudinously beneficed in Sussex and elsewhere in the beginning of the nineteenth century. He published in 1818 a solemn pamphlet entitled : " Serious Cautions and Advice to all concerned in Smuggling; setting forth the Mischiefs attendant upon that Traffic; together with some exhortations to Patience and Contentment under the Difficulties and Trials of Life. By Robert Hardy, A.M., Vicar of the united parishes of Walberton and Yapton, and of Stoughton, in Sussex; and Chaplain to H.R.H. the Prince Regent."

The author did not by any means blink the difficulties or dangers, but was, it will be conceded, far too sanguine when he wrote the following passage, in the hope of his words suppressing the trade :

" The calamities with which the Smuggler is now perpetually visited, by Informations and Fines, and Seizures, and Imprisonments, will, I trust, if properly considered, prevail upon the rich to discountenance, and upon the poor to forbear from, a traffic which, *in addition to the sin of it,* carries in its train so many evils, and mischiefs, and sorrows."

His voice we may easily learn, in perusing the history of smuggling at and after the date of his pamphlet, was as that of one crying in the wilderness. Its sound may have pleased himself, but it was absolutely wasted upon those who smuggled and those who purchased smuggled goods.

THOMAS JOHNSON

"Smugglers," he said, "are of three descriptions:

"1. Those who employ their capital in the trade;
"2. Those who do the work;
"3. Those who deal in Smuggled Articles, either as Sellers or as Buyers.

"All these are involved *in the guilt* of this unlawful traffic; but its *moral injuries* fall principally upon *the second class*.

"Smuggling," he then proceeds to say, "has not been confined to the lower orders of people; but, from what I have heard, I apprehend that it has very generally been encouraged by their superiors, for whom no manner of excuse, that I know of, can be offered. I was once asked by an inhabitant of a village near the sea whether I thought there was any harm in smuggling. Upon my replying that I not only thought there was a *great deal of harm* in it, but a *great deal of sin*, he exclaimed, ' Then the Lord have mercy upon the county of Sussex, for who is there that has not had a tub?'"

Among the ascertained careers of notable smugglers, that of Thomas Johnson affords some exciting episodes. This worthy, who appears to have been born in 1772 and to have died in 1839, doubled the parts of smuggler and pilot. He was known pretty generally as "the famous Hampshire smuggler."

As a captured and convicted smuggler he was imprisoned in the New Prison in the Borough, in 1798, but made his escape, not without suspicion of connivance on the part of the warders. That the possession of him was ardently desired by the authorities seems sufficiently evident by the fact of their offering a reward of £500 for his apprehension;

but he countered this by offering his services the following year as pilot to the British forces sent to Holland. This offer was duly accepted, and Johnson acquitted himself so greatly to the satisfaction of Sir Ralph Abercromby, commanding, that he was fully pardoned.

He then plunged into extravagant living, and finally found himself involved in heavy debts, stated (but not altogether credibly) to have totalled £11,000. Resuming his old occupation of smuggling, he was sufficiently wary not to be captured again by the revenue officers; but what they found it impossible to achieve was with little difficulty accomplished by the bailiffs, who arrested him for debt and flung him into the debtors' prison of the Fleet, in 1802. Once there, the Inland Revenue were upon him with smuggling charges, and the situation seemed so black that he determined on again making a venture for freedom. Waiting an exceptionally dark night, he, on November 29th, stealthily crossed the yard and climbed the tall enclosing wall that separated the prison from the outer world. Sitting on the summit of this wall, he let himself down slowly by the full length of his arms, just over the place where a lamp was bracketed out over the pathway, far beneath. He then let himself drop so that he would fall on to the bracket, which he calculated would admirably break the too deep drop from the summit of the wall to the ground. Unfortunately for him, an unexpected piece of projecting ironwork caught him and ripped up the entire length of his thigh. At that moment the slowly approaching footsteps of the watchman were heard, and Johnson, with agonised apprehension, saw him coming along, swinging his lantern. There was nothing for it but to lie

ESCAPE OF JOHNSON

THOMAS JOHNSON

along the bracket, bleeding profusely the while, until the watchman should have passed.

He did so, and, as soon as seemed safe, dropped to the ground and crawled to a hackney-coach, hired by his friends, that had been waiting that night and several nights earlier, near by.

Safely away from the neighbourhood of the prison, his friends procured him a post-chaise and four; and thus he travelled post-haste to the Sussex coast at Brighton. On the beach a small sailing-vessel was waiting to convey him across Channel. He landed at Calais and thence made for Flushing, where he was promptly flung into prison by the agents of Napoleon, who was at that time seriously menacing our shores with invasion from Boulogne, where his flotilla for the transport of troops then lay.

Johnson and others were, in the opening years of the nineteenth century, very busily employed in smuggling gold out of the country into France. Ever since the troubles of the Revolution in that country, and all through the wars that had been waged with the rise of Napoleon, gold had been dwindling. People, terrified at the unrest of the times, and nervous of fresh troubles to come, secreted coin, and consequently the premium on gold rose to an extraordinary height, not only on the Continent but in England as well. A guinea would then fetch as much as twenty-seven shillings, and was worth a good deal more on the other side of the Channel. Patriotism was not proof against the prospects of profits to be earned by the export of gold, and not a few otherwise respectable banking-houses embarked in the trade. Finance has no conscience.

It is obvious that only thoroughly dependable and responsible men could be employed on this business, for shipments of gold carried from £20,000 to £50,000.

Eight and ten-oared galleys were as a rule used for the traffic; the money slung in long leather purses around the oarsmen's bodies. Napoleon is said to have offered Johnson a very large reward if he would consent, as pilot, to aid his scheme of invasion, and we are told that Johnson hotly refused.

"I am a smuggler," said he, " but a true lover of my country, and no traitor."

Napoleon was no sportsman. He kept Johnson closely confined in a noisome dungeon for nine months. How much longer he proposed to hold him does not appear, for the smuggler, long watching a suitable opportunity, at last broke away, and, ignorant that a pardon was awaiting him in England, escaped to America.

Returning from that "land of the brave and the free," we find him in 1806 with the fleet commanded by Lord St. Vincent, off Brest. Precisely what services, beside the obvious one of acting as pilot, he was then rendering our Navy cannot be said, for the materials toward a life of this somewhat heroic and picturesque figure are very scanty. But that he had some plan for the destruction of the French fleet seems obvious from the correspondence of Lord St. Vincent, who, writing on August 8th, 1806, to Viscount Howick, remarks, "The vigilance of the enemy alone prevented Tom Johnstone [sic] from doing what he professed." What he professed is, unfortunately, hidden from us.

After this mysterious incident we lose sight for a while of our evasive hero, and may readily enough assume that he returned again to his smuggling

JOHNSON PUTTING OFF FROM BRIGHTON BEACH

enterprises; for it is on record that in 1809, when the unhappy Walcheren expedition was about to be dispatched, at enormous cost, from England to the malarial shores of Holland, he once more offered his services as pilot, and they were again accepted, with the promise of another pardon for lately-accrued offences.

He duly piloted the expedition, to the entire satisfaction of the Government, and received his pardon and a pension of £100 a year. He fully deserved both, for he signally distinguished himself in the course of the operations by swimming to the ramparts of a fort with a rope, by which in some unexplained manner a tremendous and disastrous explosion was effected.

He was further appointed to the command of the revenue cruiser *Fox* at the conclusion of the war, and thus set to prey upon his ancient allies; who, in their turn, made things so uncomfortable for the "scurvy rat," as they were pleased picturesquely to style him, that he rarely dared venture out of port. So it would appear that he did not for any great length of time hold that command.

But the reputation for daring and resourcefulness that he enjoyed did not seem to be clouded by this incident, for he was approached by the powerful friends of Napoleon, exiled at St. Helena, to aid them in a desperate attempt to rescue the fallen Emperor. It was said that they offered him the sum of £40,000 down, and a further very large sum if the attempt were successful. The patriotic hero of some years earlier seems to have been successfully tempted. "Every man," says the cynic, "has his price"; and £40,000 and a generous refresher formed his. For personal gain he was prepared to let loose once more the scourge of Europe.

Plans were actively afoot for the construction of a submarine boat (there is nothing new under the sun!) for the purpose of secretly conveying the distinguished exile away, when he inconsiderately died; and thus vanished Johnson's dreams of wealth. Some years later Johnson built a submarine boat to the order of the Spanish Government, and ran trials with it in the Thames, between London Bridge and Blackwall. On one occasion it became entangled in a cable of one of the vessels lying in the Pool, and for a time it seemed scarce possible the boat could easily be freed.

"We have but two and a half minutes to live," said he, consulting his watch calmly, "unless we get clear of that cable."

"Captain" Johnson, as he was generally styled, lived in quiet for many years, finally dying at the age of sixty-seven, in March 1839, in the unromantic surroundings of the Vauxhall Bridge Road.

Another smuggler of considerable reputation, of whom, however, we know all too little, was Harry Paulet. This person, who appears in some manner to have become a prisoner aboard a French man-o'-war, made his escape and took with him a bag of the enemy's despatches, which he handed over to the English naval authorities.

A greater deed was that when, sailing with a cargo of smuggled brandy, he came in view of the French fleet (we being then, as usual, at war with France), Paulet immediately went on a new tack and carried the news of the enemy's whereabouts to Lord Hawke, who promised to hang him if the news were not true.

A somewhat interesting and curious account of

A CONVERTED SMUGGLER 201

the conversion of a youthful smuggler may be found in an old volume of *The Bible Christian Magazine*. The incident belongs to the Scilly Isles.

William Gibson, the smuggler in question, was a bold, daring young man, and he, with others, had crossed over to France more than once in a small open boat, a distance of 150 miles, rowing there and back, running great risks to bring home a cargo of brandy.

In 1820, the time when William was at his best in these smuggling enterprises, St. Mary's was visited by a pious, simple-minded young woman, Mary Ann Werry by name, the first representative of the Bible Christian connexion to land on the island. The congregation were in the throes of a revival, and eager for more and more preaching, but the minister upon whom they principally relied was commercially minded, and demanded £2 for his services. The members refused to give it. "There is a woman here," said they, "we will have her to preach to us;" and, being asked, she consented, and preached from 1 Tim. iv. 8, "For bodily exercise profiteth little: but godliness is profitable unto all things, having promise of the life that now is, and of that which is to come."

We have the well-known ruling of Dr. Johnson upon the preaching of women, that it in a manner resembles a dog walking on its hind-legs: it is not done well; you only marvel that it is done at all. [N.B.—Dr. Johnson would not have favoured, or been favoured by, modern Women's Leagues.] But, at any rate, Miss Werry seems to have been a notable exception. She was eloquent and persuasive, and played upon the sensibilities of those rugged Scillonians what tune she would.

Tears of penitence rolled down the cheeks of many a stalwart man (to say nothing of the hoary sinners) that day. Among the number thus affected was William Gibson, of St. Martin's, who from that hour became a changed person. No longer did he refuse to render unto Cæsar (otherwise King George) that which was Cæsar's (or King George's). He gave up the contraband trade, and, forswearing his old companions' ways, turned to those of the righteous and the law-abiding, and became a burning and a shining light, and, as " Brother Gibson," a painful preacher in the Bible Christian communion. And thus, and in lawful fishing, with some little piloting, he continued steadfast, until his death in 1877, in his eighty-third year.

CHAPTER XIII

THE CARTER FAMILY, OF PRUSSIA COVE

IN the west of Cornwall, on the south coast of the narrow neck of land which forms the beginning of that final westerly region known as "Penwithstart," is situated Prussia Cove, originally named Porth Leah, or King's Cove. It lies just eastwardly of the low dark promontory known as Cuddan Point, and is even at this day a secluded place, lying remote from the dull high-road that runs between Helston, Marazion, and Penzance. In the days of the smugglers Porth Leah, or Prussia Cove, was something more than secluded, and those who had any business at all with the place came to it much more easily by sea than by land. This disability was, however, not so serious as at first sight it would seem to be, for the inhabitants of Prussia Cove were few, and were all, without exception, fishermen and smugglers, who were much more at home upon the sea than on land, and desired nothing so little as good roads and easy communication with the world. An interesting and authoritative sidelight upon the then condition of this district of West Cornwall is afforded by *The Gentleman's Magazine* of 1754, in which the entire absence of roads of any kind is commented upon. Bridle-paths there were, worn doubtless in the first instance by the remote original inhabitants of this region, trodden by the Phœnician traders of hoary antiquity, and unaltered in all the intervening ages.

They then remained, says *The Gentleman's Magazine,* "as the Deluge left them, and dangerous to travel over." That time of writing was the era when these conditions were coming to an end, for the road from Penrhyn to Marazion was shortly afterwards constructed, much to the alarm and disgust of the people of West Cornwall in general, and of those of Penzance in particular. Penzance required no roads, and in 1760 its Corporation petitioned, but unsuccessfully, against the extension of the turnpike road then proposed, from Marazion. That was the time when there was but one cart in the town, and when wheeled traffic was impossible outside it: pack-horses and the sledge-like contrivances known as "truckamucks" being the only methods of conveying such few goods as were required.

Under these interesting social conditions the ancient semi-independence of Western Cornwall remained, little impaired. Many still spoke the olden Cornish language; the majority of folk referred to Devonshire and the country in general beyond the Tamar as "England"—the inference being, of course, that Cornwall itself was *not* England—and smuggling was as usual an industry as tin- and copper-mining, fishing, or farming. Indeed the distances in Western Cornwall between sea and sea are so narrow that any man was commonly as excellent at farming as he was at fishing, and as expert at smuggling as at either of those more legitimate occupations. This amphibious race, wholly Celtic, adventurous, and enthusiastic, was not readily amenable to the restrictions upon trade imposed by that shadowy, distant, and impersonal abstraction called "the Government," supported by visible forces, in the way of occasional soldiers or infrequent revenue

THE CORNISH SMUGGLERS

cruisers, wherewith to make the collectors of customs at Penzance, Falmouth, or St. Ives respected.

"The coasts here swarm with smugglers," wrote George Borlase, of Penzance, agent to Lieut.-General Onslow, in 1750. Many letters by the same hand, printed in the publications of the Royal Institution of Cornwall, under the title of the " Lanisley Letters," reiterate this statement, the writer of them urging the establishment of a military force at Helston, for " just on that neighbourhood lye the smugglers and wreckers, more than about us (at Penzance), tho' there are too many in all parts of the country."

The Cornish of that time were an unregenerate race, in the fullest sense of that term, and indulged in all the evil excesses to which the Celtic nature, untouched by religion, and wallowing in ancient superstitions, is prone. They drank to excess, fought brutally, and were shameless wreckers, who did not hesitate to lure ships upon the rocks and so bring about their destruction and incidentally their own enrichment by the cargo and other valuables washed ashore. Murder was a not unusual corollary of the wreckers' fearful trade, partly because of the olden superstition that, if you saved the life of a castaway, that person whom you had preserved would afterwards bring about your own destruction. Therefore it was merely the instinct of self-preservation, and not sheer ferocity, that prompted the knocking on the head of such waifs and strays. If, at the same time, the wrecker went over the pockets of the deceased, or cut off his or her fingers, for the sake of any rings, that must not, of course, be accounted mere vulgar robbery : it was simply the frugal nature of the people, unwilling to waste anything.

Upon these simple children of nature, imbued with many of the fearful beliefs current among the savages of the South Sea islands, the Reverend John Wesley descended, in 1743. They were then, he says, a people "who neither feared God nor regarded man." Yet, so impressionable is the Celtic nature, so childlike and easily led for good or for evil, that his preaching within a marvellously short space of time entirely changed the habits of these folk. In every village and hamlet there sprang up, as by magic, Wesleyan Methodist meeting-houses; and these and other chapels of dissent from the Church of England are to this day the most outstanding features of the Cornish landscape. They are, architecturally speaking, without exception, hideous eyesores, but morally they are things of beauty. It is one of the bitterest indictments possible to be framed against the Church of England in the west that, in all its existence, it has never commanded the affections, nor exercised the spiritual influence, won by Wesley in a few short years.

It was about this period of Wesley's first visits to Cornwall that the Carter family of Prussia Cove were born. Their father, Francis Carter, who was a miner, and had, in addition, a small farm at Pengersick, traditionally came of a Shropshire family, and died in 1784. He had eight sons and two daughters, John Carter, the "King of Prussia," being the eldest. Among the others, Francis, born 1745, Henry, born 1749, and Charles, 1757, were also actively engaged in smuggling; but John, both in respect of being the eldest and by force of character, was chief of them. He and his brethren were all, to outward seeming, small farmers and fisherfolk, tilling the ungrateful land in the neighbourhood of Porth Leah, but in reality busily employed in bringing over cargoes of spirits from Roscoff, Cherbourg, and St. Malo. The origin of the nickname, "King of Prussia," borne by John Carter, is said to lie in the boyish games of the "king of the castle" kind, of himself and his brothers, in which he was always the "King of Prussia"—*i. e.* Frederick the Great, the popular hero of that age. Overlooking the cove of Porth Leah, at that time still bearing that name, he built about 1770 a large and substantial stone house, which stood, a prominent feature in the scene, until it was demolished in 1906. This he appears to have kept partly as an inn, licensed or unlicensed, which became known by his own nickname, the "King of Prussia," and in it he lived until 1807.

"Prussia Cove" is, in fact, two coves, formed by the interposition of a rocky ledge, at whose extremity is a rock-islet called the "Eneys"—*i. e.* "ynys," ancient Cornish for island. The western portion of these inlets is "Bessie's Cove," which takes its name from one Bessie Burrow, who kept an inn on the cliff-top, known as the "Kidleywink." The easterly inlet was the site of the "King of Prussia's" house. Both these rocky channels had the advantage of being tucked away by nature in recesses of the coast, and so overhung by the low cliffs that no stranger could in the least perceive what harboured there until he was actually come to the cliff's edge, and peering over them; while no passing vessel out in the Channel could detect the presence of any craft, which could not be located from the sea until the cove itself was approached.

Thus snugly seated, the Carter family throve. Of John Carter, although chief of the clan, we have few details, always excepting the one great incident of his career; and of that the account is but meagre. It seems that he had actually been impudent enough to construct a battery, mounted with some small cannon, beside his house, and had the temerity to unmask it and open fire upon the *Fairy* revenue sloop, which one day chased a smuggling craft into this lair, and had sent in a boat party. The boat withdrew before this unexpected reception, and, notice having been sent round to Penzance, a party of mounted soldiers appeared the following morning and let loose their muskets upon the smugglers, who were still holding the fort, but soon vacated it upon thus being taken in the rear, retreating to the "Kidleywink." What would next have happened had the soldiers pursued their advantage we can only surmise; but they appear to have been content with this demonstration, and to have returned whence they came, while of the revenue sloop we hear no more. Nor does Carter ever appear to have been called to account for his defiance. But if a guess may be hazarded where information does not exist, it may be assumed that Carter's line of defence would be that his fort was constructed and armed against French raids, and that he mistook the revenue vessel for a foreign privateer.

John Carter, and indeed all his brothers with him, was highly respected, as the following story will show. The excise officers of Penzance, hearing on one occasion that he was away from home, descended upon the cove with a party, and searched the place. They found a quantity of spirits lately landed, and, securing all the kegs, carried them off to Penzance and duly locked them up in the customhouse. The anger of the "King of Prussia" upon

PRUSSIA COVE

his return was great; not so great, it seems, on account of the actual loss of the goods as for the breaking of faith with his customers it involved. The spirits had been ordered by some of the gentlefolk around, and a good deal of them had been paid for. Should he be disgraced by failing to keep his engagements as an honest tradesman? Never! And so he and his set off to Penzance overnight, and, raiding the custom-house, brought away all his tubs, from among a number of others. When morning came, and the custom-house was unlocked, the excisemen knew whose handiwork this had been, because Carter was such an honourable man, and none other than himself would have been so scrupulous as to take back only his own. Yet he was also the hero of the next incident. The revenue officers once paid him a surprise visit, and overhauled his outhouses, in search of contraband. The search, on this occasion, was fruitless. But there yet remained one other shed, and this, suspiciously enough, was locked. He refused to hand over the key, whereupon the door was burst open, revealing only domestic articles. The broken door remained open throughout the night, and by morning all the contents of the shed had vanished. Carter successfully sued for the value of the property he had "lost," but he had removed it himself!

We learn something of the Carter family business from the autobiography written by Henry Carter, an account of his life from 1749 until 1795. Much else is found in a memoir printed in *The Wesleyan Methodist Magazine*, 1831. "Captain Harry" lived until 1829, farming in a small way at the neighbouring hamlet of Rinsey. He had long relinquished smuggling, having been converted in 1789, and living as a burning and a shining light in the Wesleyan communion thereafter, preaching with fervour and unction. He tells us, in his rough, unvarnished autobiography [1] that he first went smuggling and fishing with his brothers when seventeen years of age, having already worked in the mines. At twenty-five years of age he went regularly smuggling in a ten-ton sloop, with two men to help him; and was so successful that he soon had a sloop, nearly twice as large, especially built for him. Successful again, "rather beyond common," he (or "we," as he says) bought a cutter of some thirty tons, and employed a crew of ten men. "I saild in her one year, and I suppose made more safe voyages than have been ever made, since or before, with any single person." All this while, he tells us, he was under conviction of sin, but went on, nevertheless, for years, sinning and repenting. "Well, then," he continues, "in the cource of these few years, as we card a large trade with other vessels also, we gained a large sum of money, and being a speculating family, was not satisfied with small things." A new cutter was accordingly built, of about sixty tons burthen, and Captain Harry took her to sea in December 1777. Putting into St. Malo to repair a sprung bowsprit, his fine new cutter, with its sixteen guns, was taken by the French, and himself and his crew of thirty-six men were flung into prison, difficulties having again sprung up between England and France, and an embargo being laid upon all English shipping in French ports. In prison he was presently joined by his brother John; both being shortly afterwards sent on parole to Josselin. In November 1779 they were liberated, in exchange

[1] *Autobiography of a Cornish Smuggler* (Gibbings & Co., Ltd., 1900).

IN A FRENCH PRISON

for two French gentlemen, prisoners of war. The family, Captain Harry remarks, they found alive and well on their return home after this two years' absence, but in a low state, the "business" not having been managed well in their enforced absence.

It is impossible to resist the strong suspicion, in all this and other talk in the autobiography, of buying and building newer and larger vessels, that the Carters were financed by some wealthy and influential person, or persons, as undoubtedly many smugglers were, the profits of the smuggling trade, when conducted on a large scale and attended by a run of luck, being very large and amply recouping the partners for the incidental losses. But the loss of the fine new cutter, on her first voyage, at St. Malo must have been a very serious business.

After another interval of success with the smaller cutter they had earlier used, with spells ashore, " riding about the country getting freights, collecting money for the company, etc., etc.," another fifty-ton cutter was purchased, mounting nineteen guns. That venture, too, was highly successful, and " the company accordingly had a new lugger built, mounting twenty guns. Horrible to relate, Captain Harry, " being exposed to more company and sailors of all descriptions, larned to swear at times." This is bad hearing.

Obviously in those times there was a good deal of give and take going on between the Customs and those smugglers who smuggled on a large scale, and the Carters' vessels must in some unofficial way have ranked as privateers. Hence, possibly, the considerable armament they carried. The Customs, and the Admiralty too, were prepared to wink at smuggling when services against the foreign foe could be invoked. Thus we find Captain Harry, in his autobiography, narrating how the Collector of Customs at Penzance sent him a message to the effect that the *Black Prince* privateer, from Dunkirk, was off the coast, near St. Ives, and desiring him to pursue her. "It was not," frankly says Captain Harry, "a very agreeable business," but, being afraid of offending the Collector, he obeyed, and went in pursuit, with two vessels. Coming up with the enemy, after a running fight of three or four hours, the lugger received a shot that obliged her to bear up, in a sinking condition; and so her consort stood by her, and the chase was of necessity abandoned. Presently the lugger sank, fourteen of her crew of thirty-one being drowned.

In January 1788 he went with a cargo of contraband in a forty-five-ton lugger to Cawsand Bay, near Plymouth, and there met with the most serious reverse of his smuggling career, two man-o'-war's boats boarding the vessel and seizing it and its contents. He was so knocked about over the head with cutlasses that he was felled to the deck, and left there for dead.

"I suppose I might have been there aboute a quarter of an hour, until they had secured my people below, and after found me lying on the deck. One of them said, 'Here is one of the poor fellows dead.' Another made answer, 'Put the man below.' He answered again, saying, 'What use is it to put a dead man below?' and so past on. Aboute this time the vessel struck aground, the wind being about east-south-east, very hard, right on the shore. So their I laid very quiet for near the space of two hours, hearing their discourse as they walked by me, the night being very dark on the 30 Jany. 1788.

LEFT FOR DEAD

When some of them saw me lying there, said, 'Here lays one of the fellows dead,' one of them answered as before, 'Put him below.' Another said, 'The man is dead.' The commanding officer gave orders for a lantern and candle to be brought, so they took up one of my legs, as I was lying upon my belly; he let it go, and it fell as dead down on the deck. He likewayse put his hand up under my clothes, between my shirt and my skin, and then examined my head, saying, 'This man is so warm now as he was two hours back, but his head is all to atoms.' I have thought hundreds of times since what a miracle it was I neither sneezed, coughed, nor drew breath that they perceived in all this time, I suppose not less than ten or fifteen minutes. The water being ebbing, the vessel making a great heel towards the shore, so that in the course of a very little time after, as their two boats were made fast alongside, one of them broke adrift. Immediately there was orders given to man the other boat, in order to fetch her; so that when I saw them in the state of confusion, their gard broken, I thought it was my time to make my escape; so I crept on my belly on the deck, and got over a large raft just before the mainmast, close by one of the men's heels, as he was standing there handing the trysail. When I got over the lee-side I thought I should be able to swim on shore in a stroke or two. I took hold of the burtons of the mast, and, as I was lifting myself over the side, I was taken with the cramp in one of my thighs. So then I thought I should be drowned, but still willing to risk it, so that I let myself over the side very easily by a rope into the water, fearing my enemies would hear me, and then let go. As I was very near the shore, I thought to swim on shore in the course of a stroke or two, as I used to swim so well, but soon found out my mistake. I was sinking almost like a stone, and hauling astarn in deeper water, when I gave up all hopes of life, and began to swallow some water. I found a rope under my breast, so that I had not lost all my senses. I hauled upon it, and soon found one end fast to the side, just where I went overboard, which gave me a little hope of life. So that when I got there, could not tell which was best, to call to the man-of-war's men to take me in, or to stay there and die, for my life and strength were allmoste exhausted; but whilst I was thinking of this, touched bottom with my feet. Hope then sprung up, and I soon found another rope, leading towards the head of the vessel in shoaler water, so that I veered upon one and hauled upon the other that brought me under the bowsprit, and then at times upon the send of the sea, my feete were allmoste dry. I thought then I would soon be out of their way. Left go the rope, but as soon as I attempted to run, fell down, and as I fell, looking round aboute me, saw three men standing close by me. I knew they were the man-of-war's men seeing for the boat, so I lyed there quiet for some little time, and then creeped upon my belly I suppose aboute the distance of fifty yards; and as the ground was scuddy, some flat rock mixt with channels of sand, I saw before me a channel of white sand, and for fear to be seen creeping over it, which would take some time, not knowing there was anything the matter with me, made the second attempt to run, and fell in the same manner as before. My brother Charles being there, looking out for the vessel desired some Cawsand men to go down to see if they could pick up any of the men, dead or alive, not expecting to

IN HIDING 215

see me ever any more, allmoste sure I was ither shot or drowned. One of them saw me fall, ran to my assistance, and, taking hold of me under the arm, says, 'Who are you?' So as I thought him to be an enemy, made no answer. He said, 'Fear not, I am a friend; come with me.' And by that time, forth was two more come, which took me under both arms, and the other pushed me in the back, and so dragged me up to the town. I suppose it might have been about the distance of the fifth part of a mile. My strength was allmoste exhausted; my breath, nay, my life, was allmoste gone. They took me into a room where there were seven or eight of Cawsand men and my brother Charles, and when he saw me, knew me by my great coat, and cryed with joy, 'This is my brother!' So then they immediately slipt off my wet clothes, and one of them pulled off his shirt from off him and put on me, sent for a doctor, and put me to bed. Well, then, I have thought many a time since what a wonder it was. The bone of my nose cut right in two, nothing but a bit of skin holding it, and two very large cuts on my head, that two or three pieces of my skull worked out afterwards."

The difficulty before Captain Harry's friends was how to hide him away, for they were convinced that a reward would be offered for his apprehension. He was, in the first instance, taken to the house of his brother Charles, and stayed there six or seven days, until an advertisement appeared in the newspapers, offering a reward of three hundred pounds for him, within three months. He was then taken to the house of a gentleman at Marazion, and there remained close upon three weeks, removing thence to the mansion called Acton Castle, near Cuddan Point, then quite newly built by one Mr. John Stackhouse. He was moved to and fro, between Acton Castle and Marazion, and so great did his brothers think the need of precaution that the doctor who attended to his hurts was blindfolded on the way. And so matters progressed until October, when he was shipped from Mount's Bay to Leghorn, and thence, in 1789, sailed for New York. It was in New York that the Lord strove mightily with him, and he was converted and became a member of the Wesleyan Methodist communion. After some considerable trials, he sailed for England, and finally reached home again in October 1790, to his brother Charles's house at Kenneggey. His reception was enthusiastic, and he became in great request as a preacher in all that countryside. But in April 1791 he tells us he was sent for "by a great man of this neighbourhood" (probably one of those whom we have already suspected of being sleeping-partners in the Carters' business), and warned that three gentleman had been in his company one day at Helston, when one said, looking out of window, "There goes a Methodist preacher;" whereupon another answered, "I wonder how Harry Carter goes about so publicly, preaching, and the law against him. I wonder he is not apprehended." The great man warned him that it might be a wise course to return to America. "And," continues Captain Harry, "as the gent was well acquainted with our family, I dined with him, and he brought me about a mile in my way home; so I parted with him, fully determining in my own mind to soon see my dear friends in New York again. So I told my brothers what the news was, and that I was meaning to take the gent's advice. They answered, 'If you go to America, we never shall see you no

END OF CAPTAIN HARRY

more. We are meaning to car on a little trade in Roscoff, in the brandy and gin way, and if you go there you'll be as safe there as in America; likewayse we shal pay you for your comision, and you car on a little business for yourself, if you please.' So," continues this simple soul, " with prayer and supplication I made my request known unto God." And as there appeared no divine interdict upon smuggling, he accepted the agency and went to reside at Roscoff, sending over many a consignment of ardent liquors that were never intended to—and never did—pay tribute to the revenue. All went well until, in the troubles that attended the French Revolution, he was, in company with other English, arrested and flung into prison in 1793. And in prison he remained during that Reign of Terror in which English prisoners were declared by the Convention to rank with the " aristocrats " and the " suspects," and were therefore in hourly danger of the guillotine. This immediate terror passed when Robespierre was executed, July 28th, 1794, but it was not until August 1795 that Harry Carter was released. He reached home on August 22nd, and appears ever after to have settled down to tilling a modest farm and leaving smuggling to brothers John and Charles.

CHAPTER XIV

JACK RATTENBURY

WE do not expect of smugglers that they should be either literary or devout. The doings of the Hawkhurst gang, and of other desperate and bloody-minded associations of free-traders, seem more in key with the business than either the sitting at a desk, nibbling a pen and rolling a frenzied eye, in search of a telling phrase, or the singing of Methodist psalms. Yet we have, in the *Memoirs of a Smuggler*, published at Sidmouth in 1837, the career of Jack Rattenbury, smuggler, of Beer, in Devonshire, told by himself; and in the diary of Henry Carter, of Prussia Cove, and later of Rinsey, we have learned how he found peace and walked with the saints, after a not uneventful career in robbing the King's revenue of a goodly portion of its dues as by law enacted. With the eminent Mr. Henry Carter and his interesting brothers we have already dealt, reserving this chapter for the still more eminent Rattenbury, "commonly called," as he says on his own title-page (in the manner of one who knows his own worth), "The Rob Roy of the West."

We need not be so simple as to suppose that Rattenbury himself actually wrote, with his own hand, this interesting account of his adventures. The son of a village cobbler in South Devon, born in 1778, and taking to a seafaring life when nine years of age, would scarce be capable, in years of

JACK RATTENBURY

eld, of writing the conventionally " elegant " English of which his " Autobiography " is composed. But nothing " transpires " (as the actual writer of the book might say) as to whom Rattenbury recounted his moving tale, or by whose hand it was really set down. Bating, however, the conventional language, the book has the unmistakable forthright first-hand character of a personal narrative.

Before the future smuggler was born, as he tells us, his shoemaker, or cobbler, father disappeared from Beer in a manner in those days not unusual. He went on board a man-o'-war, and was never again heard of. Whether he actually " went," or was taken by a pressgang, we are left to conjecture. But they were sturdy, self-reliant people in those days, and Mrs. Rattenbury earned a livelihood in this bereavement by selling fish, " without receiving the least assistance from the parish, or any of her friends."

When Jack Rattenbury was nine years of age he was introduced to the sea by means of his uncle's fishing-boat, but dropped the family connection upon being lustily rope's-ended by the uncle as a reward for losing the boat's rudder. He then went apprentice to a Brixham fisherman, but, being the younger among several apprentices, was accordingly bullied, and left; returning to Beer, where he found his uncle busily engaging a privateer's crew, war having again broken out between England and France, and merchantmen being a likely prey.

So behold our bold privateer setting forth, keen for loot and distinction; the hearts of men and boys alike beating high in hope of such glory as might attach to capturing some defenceless trader, and in anticipation of the prize-money to be obtained by robbing him. But see the irony of the gods in their high heavens! After seven weeks' fruitless and expensive cruising at sea, they espied a likely vessel, and bore down upon her, with the horrible result that she proved to be an armed Frenchman of twenty-six guns, who promptly captured the privateer, without even the pretence of a fight : the privateering crew being sent, ironed, down below hatches aboard the Frenchman, which then set sail for Bordeaux. There those more or less gallant souls were flung into prison, whence Rattenbury managed to escape to an American ship lying in the harbour. It continued to lie there, in consequence of an embargo upon all shipping, for twelve months : an anxious time for the boy. At last, the interdict being removed, they sailed, and Rattenbury landed at New York. From that port he returned to France in another American ship, landing at Havre; and at last, after a variety of transhipments, came home again to Beer, by way of Guernsey.

He was by this time about sixteen years of age. For six months he remained at home engaged in fishing; but this he found a very dull occupation after his late roving life, and, as smuggling was then very active in the neighbourhood, and promised both profit and excitement, he accordingly engaged in a small vessel that plied between Lyme Regis and the Channel Islands, chiefly in the cognac-smuggling business. This interlude likewise soon came to an end, and he then joined a small vessel called *The Friends*, lying at Bridport. On his first voyage, in the entirely honest business of sailing to Tenby for a cargo of culm, this ship was unlucky enough to be captured by a French privateer; but Rattenbury escaped by a clever ruse, off Swanage,

JACK RATTENBURY *From an old Print.*

JACK RATTENBURY 221

and, swimming ashore, secured the intervention of the *Nancy*, revenue cutter, which recaptured *The Friends*, and brought her into Cowes that same night : a very smart piece of work, as will be readily conceded. Those were times of quick and surprising changes, and Rattenbury had not been again aboard *The Friends* more than two days when he was forcibly enlisted in the Navy by the pressgang. Escaping from the more or less glorious service of his country at the end of a fortnight, he then prudently went on a long cod-fishing cruise off Newfoundland; but on the return voyage the ship was captured by a Spanish privateer and taken to Vigo. Escaping thence, he again reached home, to be captured by the bright eyes of one of the buxom maids of Beer, where he was married, April 17th, 1801, proceeding then to live at Lyme Regis. Privateering to the west coast of Africa then occupied his activities for a time, but that business was never a profitable one, as far as Rattenbury was concerned, and they caught nothing; but, on the other hand, were nearly impressed, ship and ship's company too, by the *Alert*, King's cutter. Piloting, rather than privateering, then engaged his attention, and it was while occupied in that trade that he was again impressed and again escaped.

He then returned to Beer, and embarked upon a series of smuggling ventures, varied by attempts on the part of the pressgang to lay hold of him, and by some other (and always barren) privateering voyages. Ostensibly engaged in fishing, he landed many boat-loads of contraband at Beer, bringing them from quiet spots on the coasts of Dorset and Hampshire, where the goods had been hidden. Christchurch was one of these smugglers' warehouses, and from the creeks of that flat shore he and his fellows brought many a load, in open boats. On one of these occasions he fell in with the *Roebuck* revenue tender, which chased and fired upon him : the man who fired doing the damage to himself, for the gun burst and blew off his arm. But Rattenbury and his companions were captured, and their boat-load of gin was impounded. Rattenbury surely was a very Puck among smugglers : a tricksy sprite, at once impudent and astonishingly fortunate. He hid himself in the bottom of the enemy's own boat, and by some magical dexterity escaped when it touched shore; while his companions were held prisoners. Nay, more. When night was come, he was impudent enough, and successful enough, to go and release his friends, and at the same time to bring away three of the captured gin-kegs. In that same winter of 1805 he made seven trips in a newbuilt smuggling vessel. Five of these were successful ventures, and two were failures. In the spring of 1806 his crew and cargo of spirit-tubs were captured, on returning from Alderney, by the *Duke of York* cutter. He was taken to Dartmouth, and, with his companions, fined £100, and given the alternative of imprisonment or serving aboard a man-o'-war. After a very short experience of gaol, they chose to serve their country, chiefly because it was much easier to desert that service than to break prison; and they were then shipped in Dartmouth roads, whence Rattenbury escaped from the Navy tender while the officers were all drunk; coming ashore in a fisherman's boat, and thence making his way home by walking and riding horseback to Brixham, and from that port by fishing-smack.

Soon after this adventure he purchased a share

JACK RATTENBURY

in a galley, and, with some companions, made several successful trips in the cognac smuggling between Beer and Alderney. At last the galley was lost in a storm, and in rowing an open boat across Channel, Rattenbury and another were captured by the *Humber* sloop, and taken for trial to Falmouth and committed to Bodmin Gaol, to which they were consigned in two post-chaises, in company with two constables. Travellers were thirsty folk in those days, and at every inn between Falmouth and Bodmin the chaises were halted, so that the constables could refresh themselves. Evening was come before they had reached Bodmin, and while the now half-seas-over constables were taking another dram at the lonely wayside inn called the " Indian Queens," Rattenbury and his companions conspired to escape. Behold them, then, when ordered by the constables to resume their places, refusing, and entering into a desperate struggle with those officers of the law. A pistol was fired, the shot passing close to Rattenbury's head. He and his companion then downed the constables and escaped across the moors; where, meeting with another party of smugglers, they were sheltered at Newquay. Next morning they travelled horseback, in company with the host who had sheltered them, to Mevagissey, whence they hired a boat to Budleigh Salterton, and thence walked home again to Beer.

Next year Rattenbury was appointed captain of a smuggling vessel called the *Trafalgar*, and after five fortunate voyages had the misfortune to lose her in heavy weather off Alderney. He and some associates then bought a vessel called the *Lively*, but she was chased by a French privateer and the helmsman shot. The privateer's captain was so overcome by this incidental killing that he relinquished his prize. After a few more trips, the *Lively* proved unseaworthy, and the confederates then purchased the *Neptune*, which was wrecked after three successful voyages had been made. But Rattenbury tells us, with some pride, that he saved the cargo. In the meanwhile, however, the *Lively* having been repaired, had put to sea in the smuggling interest again, and had been captured and confiscated by the revenue officers. Rattenbury lost £160 by that business. Soon afterwards he took a share in a twelve-oared galley, and was one of those who went in it to Alderney for a cargo. On the return they were unfortunate enough to fall in with two revenue cutters, the *Stork* and the *Swallow*, that had been especially detailed to capture them; and accordingly did execute that commission, in as thorough and workmanlike fashion as possible, seizing the tubs and securing the persons of Rattenbury and two others; although the nine other oarsmen escaped. Captain Emys, of the *Stork*, took Rattenbury aboard his vessel, and treated him well, inviting him to his cabin and to eat and drink with him. Next day the smugglers were landed at Cowes.

"Rattenbury," said the genial captain, "I am going to send you aboard a man-o'-war, and you must get clear how you can." To this the saucy Rattenbury replied, "Sir, you have been giving me roast meat ever since I have been aboard, and now you have run the spit into me." He was then put aboard the *Royal William*, on which he found a great many other smuggler prisoners. Thence, in the course of a fortnight, he and the others were drafted to the *Resistance* frigate, and sent to Cork. Arrived there, our slippery Rattenbury duly escaped

JACK RATTENBURY

in the course of the following day, and was home again in six days more.

The activities of the smugglers were at times exceedingly unpatriotic in other ways than merely cheating the revenue, and Rattenbury was no whit better than his fellows. He had not long returned home when he made arrangements, for the substantial consideration of one hundred pounds, to embark across the Channel four French officers, prisoners of war, who had escaped from captivity at Tiverton. Receiving them on arrival at Beer, and concealing them in a house near the beach, their presence was soon detected and warrants were issued for the arrest of Rattenbury and five others concerned. Rattenbury adopted the safest course and surrendered voluntarily, and was acquitted, with a magisterial caution not to do it again.

Every now and again Rattenbury found himself arrested, or in danger of being arrested, as a deserter from the Navy. Returning on one of many occasions from a successful smuggling trip to Alderney, and drinking at an inn, he found himself in company with a sergeant and several privates of the South Devon Militia. Presently the sergeant, advancing towards him, said, "You are my prisoner. You are a deserter, and must go along with me."

Must! what meaning was there in that imperative word for the bold smuggler of old? None. But Rattenbury's first method was suavity, especially as the militia had armed themselves with swords and muskets, and as such weapons are exceptionally dangerous things in the hands of militiamen. "Sergeant," said he (or says his author for him, in that English which surely Rattenbury himself never employed), "you are surely labouring under an error.

I have done nothing that can authorise you in taking me up, or detaining me; you must certainly have mistaken me for some other person."

He then describes how he drew the sergeant into a parley, and how, in course of it, he jumped into the cellar, and, throwing off jacket and shirt, to prevent any one holding him, armed himself with a reaphook and bade defiance to all who should attempt to take him.

The situation was relieved at last by the artful women of Beer rushing in with an entirely fictitious story of a shipwreck and attracting the soldiers' attention. In midst of this diversion, Rattenbury jumped out, and, dashing down to the beach, got aboard his vessel. After this incident he kept out of Beer as much as possible; and shortly afterwards was successful in piloting the *Linskill* transport through a storm that was likely to have wrecked her, and so safely into port. He earned twenty guineas by this; and received the advice of the captain to get a handbill printed, detailing the circumstances of this service, by way of set-off against the various desertions for which he was liable to be at any time called to account.

Soon after this, Lord and Lady Rolle visited Beer, and Rattenbury's wife took occasion to present his lordship with one of the bills that had been struck off. " I am sorry," observed Lord Rolle, reading it, " that I cannot do anything for your husband, as I am told he was the man who threatened to cut my sergeant's guts out." Such, you see, was the execution Rattenbury, at bay in the cellar, had proposed with his reaphook upon the military.

Hearing this, and learning that Lady Rolle was also in the village, he ran after her, and overtaking her carriage, fell upon his knees and presented one of his handbills, entreating her ladyship to use her influence on his behalf, so that the authorities might not be allowed to take him. It is a ridiculous picture, but Rattenbury makes no shame in presenting it. " She then said," he tells us, " ' You ought to go back on board a man-o'-war, and be equal to Lord Nelson; you have such spirits for fighting. If you do so, you may depend I will take care you shall not be hurt.' " To which he replied, " My lady, I have ever had an aversion to [sic] the Navy. I wish to remain with my wife and family, and to support them in a creditable manner,[1] and therefore can never think of returning."

Her ladyship then said, " I will consider about it," and turned off. About a week afterwards the soldiers were ordered away from Beer, through the influence of her ladyship, as I conjecture, and the humanity of Lord Rolle.

And so Rattenbury was left in peace. He tells us that he would have now entered upon a new course of life, but found himself " engaged in difficulties from which I was unable to escape, and bound by a chain of circumstances whose links I was unable to break. . . . I seriously resolved to abandon the trade of smuggling; to take a public-house, and to employ my leisure hours in fishing, etc. At first the house appeared to answer pretty well, but after being in it for two years, I found that I was considerably gone back in the world; for that my circumstances, instead of improving, were daily getting worse, for all the money I could get by fishing and piloting went to the brewer." Thus, he says, he was obliged to return to smuggling; but we cannot

[1] By smuggling, presumably.

help suspecting that Rattenbury is here not quite honest with us, and that smuggling offered just that alluring admixture of gain and adventure he found himself incapable of resisting.

Adventures, it has been truly said, are to the adventurous; and Rattenbury's career offered no exception to the rule. There was, perhaps, never so unlucky a smuggler as he. Returning to the trade in November 1812, and returning with a cargo of spirits from Alderney, his vessel fell in with the brig *Catherine,* and was pursued, heavily fired upon, and finally captured. The captain of the *Catherine,* raging at them, declared they should all be sent aboard a man-o'-war; but a search of the smuggling craft revealed nothing except one solitary pint of gin in a bottle, the cargo having presumably been put over the side. The crew were, however, taken prisoners aboard the *Catherine,* and their vessel was taken to Brixham. Rattenbury and his men were kept aboard the *Catherine* for a week, cruising in the Channel, and then the brig put in again to Brixham, where the wives of the prisoners were anxiously waiting. Next morning, in the absence of the captain and chief officer ashore, the women came off in a boat, and were helped aboard the brig, when Rattenbury and three of his men jumped into the boat and pushed off. The second mate, who was in charge of the vessel, caught hold of the oar Rattenbury was using, and broke the blade of it, and the smuggler then threw the remaining part at him. The mate then fired; whereupon Rattenbury's wife knocked the firearm out of his hand. Picking it up, he fired again, but the boat's sail was up, and the fugitives were well on the way to shore, and made good their escape, amid a shower of bullets. They then dis-

JACK RATTENBURY

persed, two of them being afterwards retaken and sent aboard a man-o'-war bound for the West Indies; but Rattenbury made his way safely home again and was presently joined there by his wife.

The public-house was closed in November 1813, smuggling was for a time in a bad way, owing to the Channel being closely patrolled; and Rattenbury, now with a wife and four children, made but a scanty subsistence on fishing and a little piloting. In September 1814 he ventured again in the smuggling way, making a successful run to and from Cherbourg, but in November another run was quite spoilt, in the first instance by a gale, which obliged the smugglers to sink their kegs, and in the second by the revenue officers seizing the boats. Finally, on the next day a custom-house boat ran over their buoy marking the spot where the kegs had been sunk, and seized them all—over a hundred. "This," says Rattenbury, with the conciseness of a resigned victim, "was a severe loss."

The succeeding years were more fortunate for him. In 1816 he bought the sloop *Elizabeth and Kitty* cheap, having been awarded a substantial sum as salvage for having rescued her when deserted by her crew; and all that year did very well in smuggling spirits from Cherbourg. Successes and failures, arrests, escapes or releases, then followed in plentiful succession until the close of 1825, when the most serious happening of his adventurous career occurred. He was captured off Dawlish, on December 18th, returning from a smuggling expedition, and detained at Budleigh Salterton watch-house until January 2nd, when he was taken before the magistrates at Exeter and committed to gaol. There he remained until April 5th, 1827. In 1829 he says he "made an application " to Lord Rolle, who gave him a letter to the Admiral at Portsmouth, and went aboard the *Tartar* cutter. In January 1830 he took his discharge, received his pay at the custom-house, and went home.

Very slyly does he withhold from us the subject of that application, and the nature of the *Tartar's* commission; and it is left for us to discover that the bold smuggler had taken service at last with the revenue and customs authorities, and for a time placed his knowledge of the ins and outs of smuggling at the command of those whose duty it was to defeat the free-traders. It was perhaps the discovery that the work of spying and betraying was irksome, or perhaps the ready threats of his old associates, that caused him to relinquish the work.

However that may be, he was soon at smuggling again, carried on in between genuine trading enterprises; and in November 1831 was unlucky enough to be chased and captured by the Beer preventive boat. As usual, the cargo was carefully sunk before the capture was actually made, and although the preventive men strenuously grappled for it, they found nothing but a piece of rope, about one fathom long. On the very slight presumptive evidence of that length of rope, Rattenbury and his eldest son and two men were found guilty on their trial at Lyme Regis, and were committed to Dorchester Gaol. There they remained until February 1833.

Rattenbury's last smuggling experience was a shoregoing one, in the month of January 1836, at Torquay, where he was engaged with another man in carting a load of twenty tubs of brandy. They had got a mile out of Newton Abbot, at ten o'clock at night, when a party of riding-officers came up and seized the consignment " in the King's name."

JACK RATTENBURY

Rattenbury escaped, being as eel-like and evasive as ever, but his companion was arrested.

Thus, before he was quite fifty-eight years of age, he quitted an exceptionally chequered career; but his wonted fires lived in his son, who continued the tradition, even though the great days of smuggling were by now done.

That son was charged, at Exeter Assizes, in March 1836, with having on the night of December 1st, 1835, taken part with others in assaulting two custom-house officers at Budleigh Salterton. Numerous witnesses swore to his having been at Beer that night, sixteen miles away, but he was found guilty and sentenced to seven years' transportation; the Court being quite convinced, Bible oaths to the contrary notwithstanding, that he *was* at Budleigh Salterton, and did in fact take part in maltreating His Majesty's officers.

Jack Rattenbury was on this occasion cross-examined by the celebrated Mr. Serjeant Bompas, in which he declared he had brought up that son in a proper way, and " larnt him the Creed, the Lord's Prayer, and the Ten Commandments." (Perhaps also that important Eleventh Commandment, " Thou shalt not be found out ! ")

" You don't find there, ' Thou shalt not smuggle ? ' " asked Mr. Serjeant Bompas.

" No," replied Rattenbury the ready, " but I find there, ' Thou shalt not bear false witness against thy neighbour.' "

The injured innocent, like to be transported for his country's good, was granted a Royal pardon as the result of several petitions sent to Lord John Russell.

The village of Beer, deep down in one of the most

romantic rocky coves of South Devon, is nowadays a very different kind of place from what it was in Rattenbury's time. Then the home of fishermen, daring alike in fishing and in smuggling, a village to which strangers came but rarely, it is now very much of a favourite seaside resort, and full of boarding-houses that have almost entirely abolished the ancient thatched cottages. A few of these yet linger, together with one or two of the curious old stone water-conduits, and some stretches of the primitive cobbled pavements, but they will not long survive. The sole characteristic industry of Beer that is left, besides the fishing and the stone-quarrying that has been in progress from the very earliest times, is the lace-making, nowadays experiencing a revival.

CHAPTER XV

WHY THE BLOCKADE WAS ABOLISHED

To say that the Coast Blockade was in bad odour with the civil populace would be a mild way of expressing the utter detestation in which this branch of the Government service was held; and the animosity experienced by the members of the Force, combined with the irksomeness of their duties, soon caused a difficulty in obtaining volunteers for it. All sorts and conditions had to be enlisted; and these worthy fellows, finding themselves betwixt the devil and the deep sea—the chance of a flogging from their superiors, or a bullet from the smugglers—sought to evade the one, and buy off the other by accepting bribes, and then decamping.

Captain Glascock, an authoritative writer on the subject, tells us that, in consequence of the small number of men-of-war's men who could be induced to enter the force, "the roll is thus filled, for the most part—if by blue-jackets, by 'waisters' (the least intelligent of a ship's crew), or, which is more frequent, by unskilled, though hardy, Irish landsmen, whose estrangement from the sentiments, habits and religion of those placed under their surveillance seems to point them out as peculiarly adapted for a service whose basis consists in an insidious watchfulness over others, and a hostile segregation from their fellow-men."

Every year the recruiting agents had to go further

afield in search of men. Thus, on one occasion, an officer writes from Hull, expressing his delight at having discovered an unworked field, and assuring his chief that he would be able to get any number of men from that district. At last, failing other sources of supply, we find Ireland furnishing an undue proportion of recruits: not that these were bad fellows by any means—quite the contrary—and with that eagerness to handle the " base Saxon's " gold, which has ever been a notable trait of the race, these merry fellows flocked into the Force, intent on making the most of their opportunities. And, with a keen appreciation of the humour of it all, they ate the Saxon's salt, and betrayed his interests with the most charming insouciance. Yet, such is the perversity of human nature, these worthy Celts, in spite of their efforts to please, succeeded only in bringing the Blockade into worse repute than ever; while their preponderance in the Force constituted an additional grievance with the smugglers and their allies, the bulk of the coast populace, who now complained of being at the mercy of " aliens."

From time to time the feelings of " the people " found expression in print. Thus, under date June 7th, 1821, an indignant Briton wrote to the *Sussex Advertiser* :

"Sir, I cannot resist the impulse of human nature in communicating to you, for the benefit of the poor suffering men, deeds fit for the barbarous countries of Africa only in their savage state. The Coast Blockade on the Kent and Sussex coast has been made the subject of the observations and the animadversions of several members of Parliament, and these doings have been brought before the House of Commons in a variety of shapes with a view to the entire abolition of such scandals; but success has not attended these efforts because it has been very evident to Government that the system has in a great measure checked smuggling on this part of the coast, although at an enormous expense.

"The men who compose the great body are driven like slaves to their duty with the cat (whip) at their backs, and for the least deviation from the strict line of duty are thrown into the hold, ironed, and kept there until the pleasure of their Commander be known. Would you believe it? there were no less than twenty-six of these poor creatures tied up yesterday and flogged on board the ——. Their cries were piercing and reached Rye. Can people do otherwise than feel for them? They are human beings; but if brutally governed they themselves become brutal, and hence it is they attack passengers in the way described by Hon. Members, etc. . . .
"Yours truly,
"An Eye-witness."

This drew forth an indignant rejoinder, wherein the writer stigmatised the above letter as an attempt to prejudice public opinion against the Coast Blockade, with a view to its abolition—which, according to the editorial comments thereon, "would indeed be a day of Jubilee for the smugglers." It was further pointed out, in disproof of the accusations of inhumanity, that the officer commanding the vessel where the barbarities were alleged to have taken place was "of tried character and humane disposition."

Many charges of this nature were, notoriously, put in circulation for the purpose of creating an animus against the Service. Yet there was a substratum of truth in the statements. "I used to hear a deal about the Coast Blockade when I was serving in a Revenue cutter off the coast," said an old pensioner who had joined the Preventive service in 1819. "The men were known as 'McCulloch's gang,' and they would talk a lot about old 'Flogging Joey,' as they called Captain McCulloch of the *Ramillies*. He was a terrible chap for flogging. For the least thing the men would be sent off to the ship for a 'dusting down.' Every man that was brought before him knew what to expect. I have heard officers say it was a continual flog—flog—flog. Many a man swore vengeance against 'Flogging Joey'—I've heard them myself."

The system of discipline, not only in the Coast Blockade, but throughout the Navy, was, to put it mildly, harsh, at this period. For the system of terrorism which, under the false guise of discipline, had crept into the Service during the old wars—and had crystallised into a recognised custom under certain officers—was still in favour. The "cat" was in full swing, and many a poor "Block" had cause to remember the evil beast till the day of his death.

In further proof of the anxiety of the men to get clear of the Service, by hook or by crook, may be mentioned the startling fact that, in November 1826, Captain Mingaye, of H.M.S. *Hyperion*, stationed at Rye, reported a number of men for wounding themselves with a view to procuring their discharge.

Still, amongst the "scratch crews," resulting from such a system of recruiting, there were many brave

LOYALTY TO OFFICERS

and trustworthy men, who rendered valuable service to the country, even to the extent of sacrificing their lives in conflicts with smugglers; as the records of the Blockade abundantly testify. Nor was the bulk of the Force lacking in loyalty to the officers when attacked. But the loyalty of British seamen to their officers is proverbial. A somewhat touching illustration of this admirable trait was afforded many years ago at Greenock, when the smuggler was still numbered amongst the common objects of the seashore. A performance was being given at the local theatre of the once-popular "Anchor of Hope," a piece containing an exciting scene in which there is fight between a Naval officer and some smugglers—just such a scene as was being enacted, almost nightly, on the coasts of Kent and Sussex. It happened that one evening gallery and pit were filled with sailors from the Channel fleet, which had just arrived. All went well enough till the smugglers attacked the officer, and then, in a moment, the whole house was thrown into confusion. A perfect stampede of enraged tars swept on to the stage, where they fell upon the smugglers and routed them, amidst the intense excitement of the audience. It was only with the greatest difficulty that they could be made to understand that, after all, it was "only acting."

At length, feeling against the Blockade became too strong to be ignored; for although, as a branch of the Preventive Service, the Blockade had served its purpose—the smuggling trade along the south-east coast having been scotched—its methods were too rough-and-ready, not to say arbitrary, to be endured for ever. Other methods, more in harmony with the times, were now urgently called for.

Accordingly, in the year 1831, the Coast Blockade, after an eventful fifteen years' existence, was abolished, and the men paid off, their places being taken by volunteers from the Revenue cutters, and by men-of-war's men, organised and administered under a system which had been gradually developed along the seaboard, under the name of "Preventive Water-Guard"—altered, later on, to Coastguard; the several stations remaining in charge of officers of the Royal Navy, with a sprinkling of Revenue cutter commanders.

That the change had long been under consideration is evident from a letter which appeared in a Kentish paper, as far back as June 1820, to the following effect : " Sir W. J. Hope, one of the Lords of the Amiralty, accompanied by Sir John Gore, the Port Admiral at Sheerness, are on a survey of the coasts of this County and Sussex, in order to ascertain the expediency of continuing or relinquishing the establishment for the suppression of smuggling denominated the Coast Blockade : the expense being found greatly to exceed the advantages derived from it, while the plan of Preventive Stations, besides being more efficacious in its object, more than pays the whole cost of its upkeep."

On February 2nd, 1831, the *Sussex Advertiser* made the following announcement : " It appears evident it is now the serious intention of Government to do away with the Coast Blockade. The Commanding Officer of Royal Engineers has been instructed to survey the towers and redoubts and report on their state." And on March 21st : " The Coast Blockade, it is understood, will be abolished in April. The Coastguard are preparing to occupy the several stations. The measure is the reverse

END OF THE BLOCKADE 239

of calculated to excite regrets in this part of the Sussex District." On April 4th the following appeared: "The Coastguard establishment under the regulations of the Customs has commenced its duties within the last fortnight, at Hastings; and on Thursday twelve of the horse-police arrived for the performance of the interior duty for the prevention of smuggling: they are rather well-looking men and are accoutred in a manner calculated for the Service." And, finally, on May 15th, the *Hyperion*, which had been stationed for many years in Newhaven, as headquarters of the Sussex Coast Blockade, was removed, and towed round to Portsmouth.

Before all recollection of the Coast Blockade has died out, it may be well to recall the valuable services rendered by the Navy, in a new rôle, as protector of the revenue. In a time of grave national emergency, when no other disciplined force was available, the services of the "Handy Man" were invoked in aid of the Civil power, and a large force of Naval officers and seamen actively and continuously employed on shore, for a period of fifteen years, in the capacity of Coast Police. And although called on to perform duties of a most harassing, vexatious, and dangerous nature, neither the civil authorities nor even the Magistracy could be relied on for support, or even for sympathy. Both officers and men, by reason of their duties interfering with the means of livelihood of the seaboard populace, were regarded with the bitterest animosity, and subjected to the grossest calumnies and abuse: they were in frequent conflict with smugglers—fierce and reckless desperadoes of the worst type; they were liable to be shot at and brutally ill-treated, and were not seldom murdered by unknown foes—a list of men and officers who suffered death or maiming at the hands of smugglers would be astounding in its proportions. And when, by some fortunate chance, they succeeded in arresting the offenders, the appearance of officers or seamen in court was invariably signalised by an outburst of animosity on the part of the audience, which was reflected in the insulting behaviour of counsel for the defence, and too often found an echo in the conduct of the Bench. And, finally, the Coast Blockade having fulfilled its mission, and its dissolution being ordained, the men—as, alas! too often happens in John Bull's service—were sent about their business without a word of acknowledgment from the authorities, or even a valedictory sermon. History, Naval or Civil, may be searched in vain for even an allusion to the Force.